LOVE TALK

This Large Print Book carries the
Seal of Approval of N.A.V.H.

LOVE TALK

SPEAK EACH OTHER'S LANGUAGE
LIKE YOU NEVER HAVE BEFORE

DRS. LES & LESLIE PARROTT

CHRISTIAN LARGE PRINT
A part of Gale, Cengage Learning

GALE
CENGAGE Learning

Detroit • New York • San Francisco • New Haven, Conn • Waterville, Maine • London

GALE
CENGAGE Learning®

LIBRARY OF CONGRESS CATALOGING-IN-PUBLICATION DATA

Parrott, Les.
  Love talk : speak each other's language like you never have before / by Drs. Les & Leslie Parrott. — Large Print edition.
    pages cm. — (Christian Large Print originals)
  Originally published: Grand Rapids, Mich : Zondervan, c2004.
  Includes bibliographical references.
  ISBN 978-1-59415-453-9 (pbk.) — ISBN 1-59415-453-8 (pbk.) 1. Man-woman relationships—Religious aspects—Christianity. 2. Interpersonal communication—Religious aspects—Christianity. 3. Love—Religious aspects—Christianity. I. Parrott, Leslie L., 1964– II. Title.
BT705.8.P37 2013
306.7—dc23   2012044912

Published in 2013 by arrangement with The Zondervan Corporation LLC

Printed in the United States of America
2 3 4 5 6   17 16 15 14 13

To our "Friday Friends"
Bonnie and Arnie Brann
Tami and Jeff Englehorn
Lori and Brent Hagen
Sandy and Harry Hanson
Arlys and George Osborne
Joy and Jim Zorn

Your relationships are an inspiration
and we pray you'll each forever enjoy
the gift of Love Talk.

- Are you looking for a way to take your conversations to a deeper level?
- Do you know when to talk and when to clam up?
- Have your cracked the code of your spouse's communication style?
- Are you steering clear of the biggest communication mistake most couples make?
- Ever feel like your spouse is speaking a foreign language?

If so, you're ready for *Love Talk.*

CONTENTS

**PART TWO: HOW YOU SAY THE
  THINGS YOU DO**

PART THREE: ENJOYING LOVE TALK

ACKNOWLEDGMENTS

Sincere thanks . . .

To our INJOY Team: Kevin and Robin Small, Ken and Stacy Coleman, and Loran and Brenda Lichty. We can't begin to express how grateful we are for your unflinching support and enthusiasm. The heartfelt care and friendship you have given us are without compare. We continually count our blessings for knowing each of you.

To our Zondervan team: Bruce Ryskamp, Scott Bolinder, Stan Gundry, Sandy Vander Zicht, Angela Scheff, John Topliff, Greg Steilstra, Joyce Ondersma, Jackie Aldridge, Mark Hunt, John Raymond, T. J. Rathbun, and all the rest. We are humbled by your continued investment in us, and we are honored to know you not only as consummate professionals, but also as friends whose company we thoroughly enjoy.

To Sealy Yates. At long last, our dear friend, we work together, and we could not be more thrilled to have you as a partner who understands our passion and helps us achieve our mission.

To Janice Lundquist. You are inextricably woven into our lives, and we simply don't know how we could do what we do without you. After all these years, we could not be more grateful — not only for your countless efforts on our behalf, but also for the friendship we share.

To the couples who gave their support and input — whether they knew it or not — on various aspects of this manuscript along the way: Steve and Thanne Moore, Kevin and Kathy Lunn, Mark and Candi Brown, Jeff and Stacy Kemp, Rich and Linda Simmons, Scott and Debbie Daniels, George and Liz Toles, Norm and Bobbe Evans, Bill and Becky Smead, Don and Jennifer Kenney, Braxton and Kimberly Bone, Randall and Bonnie Davey, John and Cindy Trent, Rodney and Elizabeth Cox, Eric and Lisa Tooker, Doug and Margo Engberg, Tim and Tiffany Meany, and Jim and Karen Gwinn.

To Kristin (and Jeremy) Stendera whose love for our boys, John and Jackson, has given us "date nights" to practice Love Talk ourselves. What an invaluable gift you are to our family.

PROLOGUE:
CHARTING YOUR CONVERSATIONAL COURSE

We don't own a sailboat but have friends who do. And after seeing how much time and money it takes to keep one afloat, we plan on keeping it that way. Seattle, our hometown, is renowned for great sailing and all of our sailing friends have maps and charts that often cover their dining room tables. They're forever studying different passages and channels that will take them on an interesting adventure. Just before boating season opens up, they like to show us where we might go together, what we might see along the way, and what interesting ports we can visit. Charting the course gets us excited for the journey.

In much the same way, before you even turn to the first chapter of this book, we want to lay out a map of sorts that will help you know where we plan to take you. It won't take long. We're eager for you to get started, but you'll have a better journey if you know where we're going. So let's take a quick look.

Part One: Let's Talk about Talking

Our first chapter, "Can We Talk?" delves into why we felt compelled to write this book. We have a specific reason and feel you deserve to know it. Chapter 2, "Relational Lifeblood," highlights exactly what good communication can do for your love life. And we dedicate chapter 3, "Communication 101," to helping you brush up on some of the fundamentals before you dive into our new model of Love Talk. This straightforward chapter provides an easy crash course for ensuring you've thoroughly mastered the basics. These first three chapters will take your conversational craft through the inlets and marinas, some of which you will recognize, on our way to the open sea, where you'll begin to experience something you never have before.

In chapter 4, "The Foundation of Every Great Conversation," we hoist up the main sail and move out into deep water. Here we'll help you uncover something we call your personal fear factor. It has to do with what helps you feel emotionally safe when talking with your partner. And this single insight holds the potential for helping you cut through fierce waves to ride the high seas of Love Talk. We can hardly wait for you to get there.

Part Two: How You Say the Things You Do
In this section of the book, you will encounter four short chapters that each pose a question that carries a powerful punch. For how you answer each one of them will take you a step closer to revealing your unique talk style. It is this new understanding of your personal talk style that will open the doors to Love Talk.

Chapter 5 asks you to consider how you personally tackle problems, since problem solving makes up a significant portion of any couple's conversations. Whether it's figuring out how to find your destination while traveling in the car, how to get a stubborn stain out of the carpet, or how to find more minutes in your day, problem solving is a topic no couple can avoid. And understanding the chemistry of how you and your partner approach your problems — aggressively or passively — can determine how well you talk about them.

The subject of chapter 6 is how the two of you influence each other. Nearly every conversation the two of you have involves your trying to get on the same page. You may have a strong opinion about anything from a political perspective or the food at a local restaurant, and you are naturally wired to want your partner to share the same outlook. But, of course, that doesn't always happen, so you each attempt to influence the other. And you may do that more with facts or more with feelings. We'll find out for sure when we get to this chapter.

Chapter 7 asks you to consider how you react to change. Think about it: change is the one constant of every relationship, and it can consume our conversations. We change careers, we change churches, we change hairstyles, and we change our minds. Our world is in continual flux. And some of us move relentlessly into the new without ever looking back (we like the excitement and challenge of change; we like variety; we're ready and eager to move into the there and then), while others of us desperately want to hold on to the here and now (we like consistency; we like routine). Where each of you lands on this continuum will reveal a lot about your unique talk styles.

Chapter 8 will have you taking a serious look at your personal decision-making style. How do you make decisions? Are you more cautious or spontaneous? This area is another huge catalyst for conversation. Where do you want to go for dinner? Should we take a vacation or buy new carpet? Do you want to have a baby? Should we drive home on the freeway or the back roads? Every relationship is a long series of decisions. And whether you and your partner make decisions cautiously or spontaneously (and whether you make them the same way or not) reveals a great deal about your individual talk style.

Now in chapter 9 we will give you a tool for answering each of these four questions with precision. Here we will introduce you to the Love Talk Indicator — a simple instrument that just may revolutionize the way you talk to each other forever. That's a strong promise, we know. But we've come to believe it with great conviction. This powerful online self-test is sure to be an eye-opener for both you and your partner. Once you each take the Love Talk Indicator, you will receive an Individual Report of your two unique talk styles. But more important, you will receive a Couple's Report combining your two results and providing you with personalized information of how the two of you dance together in your conversation. The Love Talk Indicator will show you where you are right in step and how you can forever avoid stepping on each other's toes. We could not be more excited for you to experience the insights you will gain from the Love Talk Indicator.

Part Three: Enjoying Love Talk

Once you have identified your personal talk style, chapter 10, "Talking a Fine Line," cuts to the chase. Here we open up the secret to leveraging your talk style and enjoying the kind of heart-to-heart talks every couple longs for. We will give you a straight-shooting strategy for solving nearly 90 percent of your conversational struggles — and it's easier than you might think. It has to do with how you use your head as well as your heart (or how you should be using both) in conversations with your partner. In other words, this chapter reveals the anatomy of Love Talk.

In chapter 11, "Men Analyze, Women Sympathize," we peel away the psychobabble of gender differences and zero in on the fundamental distinction between how you and your partner speak. Men and women *are* different. But the difference doesn't have to be complicated. Once understood, our basic gender difference, coupled with our individual talk styles, becomes another tool for helping us better acquire Love Talk.

Chapter 12, "Listening with the Third Ear," points to the first duty of Love Talk — listening. We'll show you exactly what it does for a relationship, regardless of your individual talk styles, and then we'll show you how to avoid the most common mistake couples make in this area. Plus, we will give you a "mind reading" exercise you can put into practice right away and reap results from immediately.

In chapter 13, "When Not to Talk," we give some advice that may at first seem unorthodox. We show you why you sometimes need to clam up. Don't worry: it's not about shutting down your conversation; it's about how to maximize it by avoiding serious pitfalls. After surveying couples on the best times to be quiet, we've identified seven of the most important occasions when couples need to quit talking. As you'll see, this kind of silence is not only golden; it's essential to achieving the kind of conversation you long for.

Finally, in chapter 14, "Let's Talk Love," we will reveal the most important conversation you and your partner will ever have. It's a conversation most couples never even consider, and it can make all the difference as you hone and harness the power of Love Talk.

So there you have it. Fourteen chapters in all, some shorter than others, but each and every one of them designed to take you on an adventure that will change your talk life forever.

So kick off your shoes, put up your feet, and enjoy the journey.

Les and Leslie Parrott
Seattle, Washington

■ ■ ■ ■

PART 1
LET'S TALK
ABOUT TALKING

■ ■ ■ ■

What you say to your partner, and how you say it, is the single most important influence on your relationship. Your love life will sink or swim according to how well you communicate.

CHAPTER ONE:
CAN WE TALK?

WHY WE WROTE THIS BOOK

Life is deep and simple, and what our
society gives us is shallow and
complicated.

Fred Rogers

We talk a lot about talking.

In nearly every conceivable corner of
North America and in several places around
the world, Les and I have demonstrated
techniques and tools for improving a couple's communication. And it would be
impossible to add up the number of times a
couple has come into our counseling office
after a communication meltdown and given
us the common refrain: "We just don't communicate."

To say we talk a lot about talking is no
understatement. In fact, we talk so much
about it that we have been asked on numerous occasions by counselees, seminar attendees, and publishers why we have never
written a book on communication. And our

answer has remained the same: because there are already many good books out there, and until we have something ground-breaking to say on the subject, we don't feel compelled to write about it. After all, we were doing our best in our own marriage to put into practice the principles and techniques other experts had proposed. Truthfully, we weren't always doing it well either. And even when we did, we often found ourselves wanting something more — something deeper that would connect our spirits. Isn't that the goal of becoming soul mates? Communication with the one you love is more than the mere exchange of words, even if done with elegant skill. Communication, if used to full advantage, holds the promise of bringing soul mates together at a level so profound that anyone on the outside can never truly comprehend it.

So we set off to crack the code for meaningful conversation. We wanted to learn the combination for using communication to help us speak each other's language like we never had before. At least, that's the way Les puts it. I think of it more as uncovering some of the deep mystery of male-female relationships — knowing this relationship is too complex and multifaceted to be codified. Of course, we'll get to our differing styles of word choice and metaphor (as well as yours) later on in this book. The point is that for more than a decade we have been on the lookout for this seemingly illusive secret — something we both longed for. We were determined not to get sidetracked by anything shallow or complicated. We were in pursuit of a deep and simple plan that would move our communication from good to great. If we discovered a new technique or a clever method along the way, we took note, but new techniques were not our primary goal. We wanted to get to the heart of the matter. We wouldn't settle for a mere handful of golden nuggets; we were in search of the mother lode. We wanted to find the means to becoming more understanding and better understood. We were in pursuit of *the* secret that would unlock a full supply of the very lifeblood of a meaningful relationship.[1]

What great delight it is to see the ones we love and then to have speech with them.
                                    Vincent McNabb

And we found it. The book you hold in your hands is the result of many years of research, and it will show you exactly what we discovered: a deep and simple plan for everything a loving conversation has to offer. We call it Love Talk.

What's the Goal?

Allow us to come alongside you for a moment and imagine where you are. You may be at the beginning stages of a dating relationship or on the edge of commitment, about to be engaged. You may be in the first few years of your marriage, or you may have decades under your belt. You may be in a second marriage, struggling to blend a family. Perhaps you're in a small group with other couples or a class that's dedicated to improving your love life. Wherever you find yourself at the moment, we want you to know that we have written and rewritten these words with you in mind. We have reviewed each chapter, each paragraph, while putting ourselves, as best we can, in your place. We want this book to be an effective tool for any and every couple who wants to find a better way of speaking each other's language.

We want you to thoroughly understand one another and your specific communication styles. We don't want to simply hand off a few new techniques you can try on for a while to see if they work; we want to give you an experience that will take you to a new level of communication, deeper for you than it has ever been before. After reading this book, we want you to enjoy the incomparable comfort of saying what's on your mind and revealing what's in your heart. We are going to give you a means for communicating like you never have before.

So with this goal in mind, we want to give you our first challenge. After working with many couples, we have come to believe with great conviction that you are far more likely to improve your situation and meet your personal goals for communication if you clearly articulate them. That's why we want to encourage you — right now — to take just a few minutes to write down a sentence or two describing your personal goal in reading this book. How would you like your communication to be different as a result of the time you will spend with us in these pages? Make it specific and concrete. For example, if you are dating, you may want to have a conversation that allows you to talk freely about a difficult topic that has been on your heart. Or if you are married, you may want to be able to talk to each other about disciplining your children without having a heated debate. Or maybe you simply want to enjoy a leisurely conversation over dinner together three days a week. You get the point. The first *Love Talk Workbook* exercise will give you a helpful structure for noting your goals and show you more specifically how you can chart your progress.

All the exercises we will be pointing you to in this book are found in the accompanying *Love Talk* workbooks — one workbook for men and another for women, so you can complete the exercises independently and then discuss them. These workbooks are available at your local bookstore or at www .RealRelationships.com.

Exercise 1: Getting Where You Want to Go

Before moving further into this chapter, we urge you to take inventory of where you are and where you want to be. This initial workbook exercise will set the stage for the work you do in chapters to come.

We have deliberately whittled this book down to a manageable size. We aren't interested in overloading you with information and don't want you to get bogged down or weary along the way. So we're shooting straight: once you and your partner discover the secret of Love Talk, we believe your conversations will never be the same.

CHAPTER TWO:
RELATIONAL LIFEBLOOD
WHY COMMUNICATION IS
VITAL TO YOUR LOVE LIFE

To listen closely and reply well is the highest perfection we are able to attain in the art of conversation.
Francois de La Rochefoucauld

"Does Jackson have sun in his eyes?"

"No, I think he's just a little fussy," I responded while glancing at our son in the rearview mirror. "What are we going to have for dinner tonight?"

"Dinner! Your son is in agony, and you're thinking about food?" Leslie didn't have to ask this rhetorical question. I got the message loud and clear once she unbuckled her seat belt and climbed into the backseat of the car to shield our second son from the slightest ray of any potential light as we rounded a corner.

"Are you okay?" I asked. Leslie simply rolled her eyes. "If you wanted me to adjust his visor, why didn't you just ask me?"

"I did."

"No," I said with the confidence of a high-priced attorney. "You asked me if the sunlight was bothering Jack."

"Exactly. I asked you to reach back and make sure the sun wouldn't bother him by pulling up the visor. Apparently I have to spell it out!"

"Not a bad idea," I mumbled under my breath.

"What?" Leslie asked.

No response. I just kept my eyes on the road as if driving had suddenly demanded my undivided attention.

"Did you say something?" she asked again.

"No. Not really."

By now, our baby had stopped crying (I suppose that had something to do with the visor on his car seat), and Leslie and I both sat still.

A couple of minutes passed when Leslie uttered a single word: "Tacos."

I hesitated. Then I caught her eye in the rearview mirror. "Sounds good," I said with a smile.

This conversation between us occurred yesterday afternoon on a carefree drive to a park not far from our house. We were under no stress. No traffic jam. Just a cheery little outing with our kids, or so we thought. But why the hiccup in our communication? How could a little exchange of words become mangled so quickly?

> I would rather be disagreed with by someone who understands me, than to be agreed with by someone who does not understand me.
> James D. Glasse

Truth is, we know better than to let our conversation get tangled up with crossed communiqués. After all, we've been married for two decades. We counsel other couples. We give national marriage seminars. Trust me, we have the tools. We know the techniques.

So how could we let a seemingly simple conversation fall apart? Sure, we brought it back around quickly and moved forward — at least on this occasion. Jackson's needs were taken care of, and we were having tacos for dinner. Case closed. The miscommunication was a tiny smudge on the big picture of our day. It was quickly filed away as a minor blunder, never to be brought up again. Or was it?

Studies have shown that these seemingly insignificant missteps in communication have a more important effect than you might know. Each message that breaks down, no matter how small, inscribes a little note on your relationship: "My partner doesn't understand me." It may not be conscious or articulated, but it is felt. And when a couple suffers enough of these breakdowns over time, isolation and loneliness are bound to creep in.

Conversely, when you and your partner are communicating well, when you are humming along and in sync, there is an indelible inscription on your relationship that is priceless: "I am known and understood." That feeling of being on the same page, of speaking each other's language — fluently — is what this book is all about.

More than any other measure, couples gauge the depth of their connection by the satisfaction of their conversations. And rightly so. It is an excellent barometer of our bond. But some couples routinely underestimate the importance of talk. "Our communication is fine," a wife may say. "The problem is that he's too attached to his mother." Okay. Maybe that's a factor. And psychoanalyzing relational dynamics has its place, but trust us when we say that exploring how we talk to each other is more responsible for finding solutions than any armchair analysis. Some people just can't believe that something as simple as understanding our talk styles (which we get to in Part Two) can transform a relationship. But it can. Study after study indicates that improving your communication increases the quality of your relationship more than anything else you do.

Let's Get Real

"I can't stand it when you give me that look," I said to Les as I was rummaging through my purse to find a scrap of paper with some driving directions.

"What look?" Les asked with one hand on the steering wheel and the other fumbling with his cell phone.

"You know exactly what look — the one that says I'm dim-witted," I snapped back.

"I didn't say a thing," Les responded.

"Exactly," I said. "Your face said it for you."

"I just thought you might know where we were supposed to go since you said you'd get the directions."

"Yes, but you're so condescending when you look at me that way."

"I could say the same about you, but —" Les's sentence fell off as we both saw an exceptionally large sign just a few yards from our car: "Becoming Soul Mates with Relationship Experts Drs. Les and Leslie Parrott."

It was Saturday morning in Portland, Oregon, where several hundred couples had gathered and paid good money to hear what "the experts" had to say about love and relationships.

"Just keep driving," I said to Les. And he did. We circled that block at least four times before we could get our act — and I do mean act (at least at the outset) — together.

We are the first to admit that our communication as a couple is not perfect. Far from it. That day in Portland happened eight years ago, but we can still be as vulnerable as any other couple to snide remarks and miscommunication. Thankfully, however, those moments are not as frequent as they once were.

> Once a word has been allowed to escape, it cannot be recalled.
> Horace

Obviously, we can't promise to steer you forever away from inane conversations that break down from time to time, but in this book we do intend to show you exactly how you can cultivate positive dialogue that surpasses the negative. We intend to share with you the communication secret we call Love Talk — and it is something you won't find in any other book. We've been developing this approach for many years, and it has done nothing short of revolutionize our relationship and the hundreds of couples we have taught it to along the way.

Before we get started, however, we want to quickly assess your communication IQ with the workbook exercises. This will give you a baseline upon which to measure your success as you proceed through these pages. Here at the outset, we also want to underscore how vital quality communication is to your relationship and show you how bad communication can spoil a good relationship. We'll conclude this brief chapter with an explanation of why so many talking techniques can fall short. In other words, if you've tried to practice a communication method or procedure that didn't deliver, we'll show you why.

Ready to Talk and Nothing to Say

It's date night. After a week of juggling schedules, wrestling traffic, paying bills, and all the rest, the two of you are headed out for a meal together, just the two of you. Or maybe you're going to catch a flick and unwind with conversation over a cup of coffee at Starbucks. Whatever the plan, you both finally sit down to (drumroll) converse. It's your chance to connect, chat, discuss, catch up.

"So how was your day?" you ask your husband.

"Good. It was good."

"What happened?"

"Same old stuff, really. Nothing new."

"Isn't it great to finally have some time to ourselves?" you say, undaunted by the false start to what is certain to be a meaningful heart-to-heart conversation.

"Yeah," he says as he looks around the restaurant.

"You seem distracted."

"No. Not at all. I just wondered if the game was over and who won."

"Okay," you say slowly, raising the pitch of your voice as you drag out the word.

He picks up on the message and attempts to turn it around. "It doesn't really matter who won the game. Let's talk."

That's when you look at each other blankly and wonder what you have to talk about. There is a plethora of words primed and ready for a great exchange somewhere within your vocal chords, and yet nothing comes out. So you sip your coffee and wrack your brain for the start of a meaningful conversation.

If you didn't already know, let's put it on the table: The number one problem couples report is "a breakdown in communication." And with good reason. Whether a relationship sinks or swims depends on how well partners send and receive messages, how well they use their conversations to understand and be understood. Think about it. If you are feeling especially close to your partner, it is because you are communicating well. Your spirits are up. Your love life is full. You are in tune. And when communication falls flat, when you feel stuck and you're talking in circles, relational satisfaction drops. Communication, more than any other aspect of your relationship, can either buoy relational intimacy or be the deadweight of its demise.

How Bad Communication Can Spoil a Good Relationship

Time and again, we have seen faulty communication lines pull down an otherwise sturdy relationship: both partners struggle to convey what they want or need in the relationship, never realizing they are speaking a language the other does not comprehend. Over the disappointment, the partners erect defenses against each other, becoming guarded. They stop confiding in each other, wall off parts of themselves, and withdraw emotionally from the relationship. They can't talk without blaming, so they stop listening.

It is difficult to exaggerate the importance of communication in any relationship, but especially marriage. Almost all couples (97 percent) who rate their communication with their partner as excellent are happily married, compared to only 56 percent who rate their communication as poor. The poll concluded: "In an era of increasingly fragile marriages, a couple's ability to communicate is the single most important contributor to a stable and satisfying marriage."[1]

Love relationships maintain themselves linguistically: when we talk to our partner, we search for signs of love but become attuned to signs of disapproval. After all, our relationship is the peg on which we hang our sense of who we are. In other words, our very identity is at stake when we are not feeling understood and loved by our partner. This is the crux of how bad communication spoils a good relationship. Little conversations, piled one on top of the other, can easily tip the scales toward feeling misunderstood — especially when we become attuned to any potential sign of disapproval.

> The character of a man is known from his conversations.
>
> Menander

Perhaps the most painful example of this dynamic is found in a message that combines caring with criticism.

"Do you really need another bowl of ice cream?" Olivia asks Michael as he fumbles around in the freezer.

"You bet I do," he replies (as if to say, "If I wasn't sure before, I certainly am now").

"Why do you always watch what I eat?"

"Because I love you," she says with sincerity. "I'm just looking out for you."

It's a simple question about ice cream, right? Not exactly. While she is focused on helping him improve his diet, he is focused on being criticized for eating too much — and he ends up feeling judged, distant, and misunderstood.

Or consider how the same thing happens when the roles are reversed for this couple:

"The towels in our bathroom are overdue for a wash," Michael observes.

Regardless of how it's intended, what Olivia hears is "You aren't doing a very good job of keeping this house clean."

The impression of disapproval comes not from the message, the words spoken, but from Olivia's attunement to disapproval. So the seemingly simple observation leads her to feel she can't get approval from the person whose approval means the most.

So we'll say it again: love relationships maintain themselves linguistically. But a mere exchange of information — no matter how well it is communicated — is not enough to keep a love relationship alive.

Staying Informed ≠ Staying In Touch

In the middle of the nineteenth century, Ralph Waldo Emerson registered a lyrical complaint about the oppressive force of material goods: "Web to weave and corn to grind; Things are in the saddle and ride mankind." Talk about your sensitive poet! If Emerson found such modest machinery as corn grinders dehumanizing, how would he handle our modern-day gadgetry? Today we are tethered to computers and cell phones and pagers. We can make calls from airplanes and hold meetings in real time involving members in several cities without anyone leaving home. The advances in technological communication are nothing less than astonishing. Yet all these tools have done nothing to ensure better communication between people, let alone couples.

As I (Les) type these words into my computer, a little electronic flag near the bottom of my screen tells me that Leslie is on her computer in another room of the house. Since her laptop is networked wirelessly, she could even be in the garden. She has sent me a message, and I'll read it at my first convenience. If I'm in a meeting and want to send her a discreet message, I can key it into my cell phone and press enter, and she sees it immediately. More

44

than ever, it is easy to stay informed. But being informed is not the same as communicating, at least not for soul mates. Communication for couples still requires a set of skills that no technology can ever replace. We'll say it again: good communication requires fundamental, easily learned skills (more on this in the next chapter). They are essential for learning how to talk so your mate will listen and how to listen so your mate will talk. But skills are not enough.

Our guess is that you know just what we mean. Since you recognize the inherent value of good communication (you wouldn't be reading this book if you didn't), you have probably read other books on the subject or attended seminars that have given you techniques to help you improve it. But if you are like us and other couples we have counseled, you may have felt the techniques didn't always deliver on their promise. Perhaps you felt a bit robotic or phony when you were attempting to follow the proper procedure. If so, we need to talk.

Why Talking Techniques Can Fall Short
We were sitting at the airport waiting for a plane when a woman approached us. "You're Les and Leslie, right?" She went on

> ## Exercise 3: Your Current Couple-Communication Strengths
>
> It is often helpful to consider what works and what doesn't, in specific terms, for you and your partner. This brief exercise in the men's and women's workbooks will help you highlight what's working well in your communication journey, and it will also show you how to post warning signs on any paths you're traveling that won't lead you to your desired destination.

to tell us that she and her husband had heard us speak in Houston a couple of months before. She said some kind words about the experience and then confessed: "We've been doing the communication exercises you demonstrated, but they don't work."

Her statement was heartfelt. Not accusatory. She was simply puzzled because she was practicing what she knew to do and not seeing results. She showed us how she would "reflect back" her partner's feelings, how she would clarify his content and rephrase it. After a few minutes, however, it was clear to us what was happening: She was so intent on *doing* communication, she was neglecting to *be* a good communicator. In other words, she was doing the right things for the wrong reasons. She wasn't genuine. She was more concerned about practicing a method than she was about understanding her mate. And he saw right through it. Your partner would too.

Everyone has a built-in radar detector for phoniness, spotting fabricated feelings and insincere intentions long before they are openly expressed. Your partner will not trust you if he or she feels you are not genuine. Without genuineness, little else in marriage matters — especially when it comes to communication.

How is genuineness expressed? Not in words. What you say to your partner is far less important than how you say it — with a smile, a shrug, a frown, or a glare. Consider this: nonverbal communication accounts for 58 percent of the total message. Tone of voice makes up 35 percent of the message. The actual words you say account for only 7 percent of the total message.[2]

Consider two scenarios involving the exact same sentence by a husband: "I sure hope we get to the restaurant on time."

In the first scene, the husband sighs heavily, rolls his eyes, then says this sentence slowly while leaning against the bedroom doorframe with his arms crossed as his wife holds up different earrings to her ears in front of the mirror.

In the second scene, the husband says this very same sentence as his wife is doing the very same thing. But he has excitement in his voice as he stands behind her and gently squeezes her shoulders with his hands and smiles at her in the mirror.

Same words, so it's the same meaning, right? Hardly. The words are only a fraction of the message.

Genuineness is expressed in your tone and nonverbal behavior, your eyes and your posture. Research has found that men and women are accurate interpreters of their partner's nonverbal communication. An acquaintance may not notice a subtle change in your facial expression, but your partner will.

You can use all the communication techniques in the world, but if you aren't genuine, they won't work. Authenticity is something you are, not something you do. It comes from the heart, not the hands.

As a psychologist (Les) and a marriage and family therapist (Leslie), we can tell you that almost every communication problem for soul mates can be traced to a lack of genuineness. It is the bedrock of good communication.

Exercise 4: Let's Get Real

Since genuineness is paramount to good communication, we want to provide both of you with a brief exercise to help you tap into this important quality within yourself. Take a moment to do this exercise in your workbooks and discover how you best express your authenticity.

Maybe you don't want to hear this. Maybe you simply want a new verbal strategy, more techniques and tools. We'll get to that. But we have to make this abundantly clear: who you are is more important than what you do when it comes to communication. You can practice great communication techniques and still end up sounding like nothing more than a "clanging cymbal." That's how Paul puts it in his famous love poem in his letter to the Corinthians.[3]

As an exercise in internalizing this popular piece of Scripture, we once wrote a personal interpretation of it with a new twist. In part it said, "If I go to marriage seminars and read marriage books to learn new verbal strategies but am not genuine, I'm nothing more than an annoying tape recorder that replays my partner's messages."

You get the point. The remainder of this book is predicated on the idea that you *genuinely* want to understand your partner. If you don't, you won't find a book on the planet that can help you communicate better. But if you are truly invested in taking your communication to a whole new level, you are ready for Love Talk.

CHAPTER THREE:
COMMUNICATION 101
BRUSHING UP ON THE BASICS

> Good communication is as
> stimulating as black coffee.
> Anne Morrow Lindbergh

We recently read the story of a columnist for the *Seattle Times,* Mark Trahant, and his traditional wedding to a Navaho woman. As was customary, tribal couples crowded into their Hogan to offer counsel to the newlyweds. One man cleared his throat as if to speak, but at that very moment his wife kneed him in the back. So he kept silent. Later he again cleared his throat but again felt his wife's probing knee. It happened a third time.

As the guests filed out, the wife with the knee asked her husband, "Why did you say nothing?"

"I was going to, but each time I was about to speak, I thought you didn't want me to."

"I nudged you three times to get you to speak," she protested. "What would you have said?"

"I would have spoken of the importance of communication in marriage."

Sometimes, a couple needs to get back to the basics. The fundamentals. After all, communication is so often taken for granted. Researchers estimate that we spend 70 percent of our waking hours communicating with others — speaking, listening, reading, or writing. Thirty-three percent of that time is devoted to talking and 42 percent to listening. We communicate more than just about any other human activity. And yet we rarely have the skills we need to maximize its effectiveness, which is why we devote this chapter to giving you the basic tools for good conversations.

Now if you already have a lock on the basics of a good conversation, feel free to move quickly through this chapter or skip it altogether. No guilt. Just move to the next chapter. But if, like many of us, you'd like a quick brushup on the fundamentals, read on.

We Really *Need* to Communicate

Nothing destroys like isolation. The military men confined to solitary cells in the infamous Hanoi Hilton understood this like few others. "Communication sustained us," says ex-Air Force pilot Ron Bliss. "It sounded like a den of runaway woodpeckers," he said about the code they developed for sending messages. The North Vietnamese never mastered the code, which laid out the alphabet on a simple 5-by-5 grid (omitting K, for which C was used).

```
A  B  C  D  E
F  G  H  I  J
L  M  N  O  P
Q  R  S  T  U
V  W  X  Y  Z
```

The soldiers tapped first the line, then the letter in that line. Thus the letter *B* would be *tap . . . tap tap.* The code flowed so fluently that the men told one another jokes; kicks on the wall meant a laugh. Every Sunday, at a coded signal, the men stood and recited the Lord's Prayer and the Pledge of Allegiance. Their communication literally kept them alive.

And that's exactly what good communication does for a relationship. It keeps it alive. It sustains a connection between soul mates. A couple literally *needs* to converse — a meaningful relationship depends on it. We can't tell you how many couples have come to our counseling office on the brink of a breakup because they "just can't communicate." Their words have dried up. Of course, what they really mean is that they just don't know how to communicate in a way that is meaningful and healthy. Two people, even at an apparent and long-standing impasse, can always learn to talk to each other and break through their gridlock. And more often than not, the breakthrough comes in revisiting the fundamentals of communication.

> When I think of talking, it is of course with a woman. For talking at its best being an inspiration, it wants a corresponding divine quality of receptiveness, and where will you find this but in a woman?
> Oliver Wendell Holmes

Of course, some couples have a more unique situation — one of them (typically the man) may be what we call a "silent partner." This is the person who tends not to talk much in general, so we have devoted a special chapter in the appendix of this book to address this scenario. If you already know your relationship could get a boost from help in this area, you many want to peruse this appendix after completing this chapter.

But for most couples, communication comes back to the basics. So let's start at the very beginning, zeroing in on what communication fundamentally requires. And first on the list? Your time.

Making Time for Talk

In 1997, the Washington Capitals were one of the hottest hockey teams on ice, skating their way into the Stanley Cup finals. But by the fall of 1999, they had slipped to the brink of disaster with one of the worst records in the NHL. Coach Ron Wilson decided drastic measures were necessary and quickly changed their strategy. Yet injuries abounded, and the losses mounted. The team couldn't figure out what was wrong.

Just before Christmas, the team embarked on a late-night, seven-hour flight home from Vancouver and did what they typically do on a flight of that duration: They popped in a movie to pass the time. To unwind. To lick their wounds. That's when the unexpected happened. The VCR froze — there would be no movie on this flight.

As the plane winged its way through the

evening sky, one by one the players started talking with each other. They talked strategy. Obstacles. Key plays. Out of necessity, they rediscovered the ancient art of conversation. By the time the plane touched down, the Capitals had picked apart their game and knew what needed to be done.

In the weeks that followed, they became virtually unstoppable, going on an eleven-game winning streak. Team goaltender Olaf Kolzig reflected, "Maybe it was fate the VCR didn't work. It gave us a chance to just roam about the plane and talk. It was a good way to clear the air."

Time and talk are always a winning combination. Most of us have an automatically advancing speed rheostat, and every year the treadmill spins faster. Husbands and wives, for example, have become out-of-breath companions, racing around to catch up with their schedules (as well as their children's). Even our sentences are peppered with such words as *time crunch, fast food, rush hour, frequent flyer, expressway,* and *rapid transit.* We use cell phones managed by Sprint, do our finances on Quicken, schedule appointments on a DayRunner, diet with SlimFast. Whew! We're all in a hurry and anything that slows us down becomes the equivalent of road-kill —

including our most important relationships.

> It is difficult not only to say the right thing in the right place, but far more difficult to leave unsaid the wrong thing at the tempting moment.
>
> George Sala

That's why we are compelled to state the obvious: good communication requires time to talk. A good conversation simply doesn't happen while traveling at breakneck speed. So cure your hurry sickness, take a deep breath, and obey the speed limit of human connection. If you want to improve your communication, you must ruthlessly eliminate hurry from your conversations. You can accomplish this the old-fashioned way: sitting still without multitasking, lingering over your dinner conversation, taking advantage of a quiet house when the kids are in bed before you fall asleep, turning off the radio when you are driving in the car, or turning off the TV when it is simply background noise — so you can talk.

It also helps to anticipate your talk time (like over a meal at a restaurant) by considering topics you'd like to bring up when you know you will both be in a relaxed and calm space. You may also want to identify where and when you have your best talks. Is it over a cup of coffee in the morning? At brunch on a lazy Saturday? In the car when you have a relatively long drive together? These are times you want to protect and prioritize.

You get the idea. Oh, and one more practical way to eliminate hurry from your conversations? Drop this sentence from your personal lexicon: "Get to the point." That's a tough one for many of us, but do your best to keep it at bay.

The Three Levels of Couple Communication

Communication between partners can be broken down into three levels according to authors Robert and Rosemary Barnes. The goal, however, is to get to the third level on a regular basis. Let's take a quick look at each.

The Grunt Level

This is the shallowest level of communication, involving the obligatory comments that do little more than make your presence known. Some couples fall into this pattern when arriving home from work. They say

> **Exercise 5: Finding the Time to Talk**
>
> It is one of the greatest life hurdles we ever encounter: finding time for things that matter most — like good conversations. In this simple workbook exercise, we have you both take a good look at your time, how much you have, how you use it, and where it may be slipping away. And, most important, how to recapture it. Take a moment right now to find the time of your life with this workbook exercise.

the required things but never really listen to one another. The requisite "How ya doing?" is met with the predictable "Fine." That's it. Couples at this level don't expect it to go any further. And that's fine, for a while. Actually, the grunt level can provide a degree of comfort — not having to say much, simply enjoying each other's presence. But sadly, if this goes on too long, a couple will begin to drift and eventually not even know each other anymore.

The Journalist Level

Here a couple talks about facts and opinions. They may talk about politics, people, church, movies, or sports. "I sure thought

> Let your conversation be always full of grace.
>
> Colossians 4:6

that sermon was long today, and did you notice the temperature in that building?" They voice their opinions, explore the facts, but that's where it stops. This kind of communication has its place but lacks intimacy or real connection. Just reporting and discussing won't always bring you closer together.

The Feelings Level

A couple reaches this level when each partner feels safe enough to share areas of weakness or feelings that may put him or her in a bad light. In other words, they let their guard down. They reveal their heart and speak their mind, knowing they will be understood and accepted. At this level, couples ask each other for input and help. They share their insecurities and their dreams. They feel known and connected, deep down in their soul. This is the result of Love Talk. And while we can't always expect to communicate at this level, we can generally enjoy the safety of this level more often than we think.

Exercise 6: Your Three Levels of Communication

We all long to connect with our partner primarily at the feelings level. But let's be honest, in our hurried lifestyles those times are often few and far between, though they don't have to be. We can enjoy more heart-to-heart conversations in spite of our hurry sickness, and this exercise in the workbooks will show you how.

Attending Skills

If a couple is ever to make it to the feelings level of communication and linger there, it will be because they have a handle on *attending*. This is the word communication specialists use to describe the physical and psychological attention you give to your partner during a conversation. These are the nonverbals that can make or break your connection.

Effective physical attending takes place when your involvement is visibly apparent to your partner. The following are several components of good attending:

Eyes: Eye contact is key to staying connected. This doesn't mean you stare. It's a natural look throughout the conversation.

Posture: Usually, when you are listening, you should lean slightly toward your partner, as long as you're relaxed. Your posture should also stay open and receptive (not crossing your arms).

Gestures: If you are fidgety, drum your fingers on the table, or sneak glances at your watch, you are conveying a message, intentionally or not, of being uninterested. Just remember to avoid gestures that might be distracting.

Environment: A space that promotes good conversation provides proximity to one another, a degree of privacy, and a pleasant mood. In other words, not in front of the TV. Sorry.

The underlying message to your partner when you are attending well is that what he or she says matters. Once you've got this down, the next task is to make sure you accurately understand the words you are hearing.

Clarifying Skills

Take a second to decipher this phrase:

Love
isnowhere

How do you read the two lines? Some see "Love is nowhere." Others read "Love is now here." And every once in a while, someone sees "Love I snow here." In the same way, we may see an entirely different meaning from the one our partner intends.

When absurd misunderstandings happened between Abbott and Costello, the famous comedy team, the whole nation chuckled. But in a romantic relationship, being misunderstood is no laughing matter. Misunderstanding does not result from not hearing the words but from not clarifying the meaning of the words. The five hundred most commonly used words in the English language carry over fourteen hundred different meanings — an average of nearly three meanings for each word!

Consider this example: Sherry walks into the family room and says to her husband, Keith, "I feel like such a failure when this place isn't picked up, and I know your mom is dropping by tomorrow."

Pretty straightforward, right? What's to

clarify? Well, what is she saying exactly? It may not be what you think. Consider these clarifications:

Keith: Sounds like you think the house is a mess.

Sherry: Oh, no. It's always going to be like this until the boys are older.

or

Keith: You sound a little depressed; are you alright?

Sherry: I'm not depressed. I think I'm mostly upset that my boss wouldn't give me tomorrow off.

or

Keith: Is my mom's visit stressing you out?

Sherry: Actually, I'm thrilled that she'll be here. I just wish I had the energy to vacuum tonight.

See how it works? A simple inquiry to make sure you understand the message goes a long way. Clarification keeps you from jumping to conclusions. It ensures you stay on track, dealing accurately with the intended message.

Keith in this example could have easily jumped to a number of conclusions, thinking he knew exactly what his partner was saying: *She wants me to clean this room,* or *she wishes my mom wasn't dropping by,* or *she's feeling depressed.* And in each conclusion he would have been wrong. That's why this fundamental skill is so essential.

> Never miss a good chance
> to shut up.
>
> Will Rodgers

By the way, as long as you are genuinely interested in understanding what your partner is saying, you can be dead wrong on your clarification, and it will still work. Notice that in all three attempts to clarify above, Keith wasn't ever directly on target. That doesn't matter. What matters is that Sherry had the opportunity to clarify her statement.

Steering Clear of Advice

Carl Jung said that advice seldom hurts any of us because we so rarely take it seriously. The latter part of his statement may be true, but countless couples can attest to the falsity of the first part. Advice can wreak havoc on marital conversation.

Giving advice to your partner is like garlic — a little bit goes a long way. When we make suggestions to our partner before we have truly earned the right to do so (i.e., when they ask for it), we may believe we are being helpful, but we're not.

Advice-giving can actually make your partner feel worse because she cannot or is not ready to follow through on it. This can instill terrible pangs of guilt. The biblical advice that Job's friends gave him in his time of affliction, for example, served only to make poor Job more miserable.[1]

Trigger-happy advice is costly. Once your partner hears your "words of wisdom," he may turn you off and say, "I don't want to talk about it anymore!" or "You just don't understand." Unwelcome advice clogs the flow of genuine feelings and eventually puts a halt to any meaningful conversation.

Devising a Cheat Sheet

Well, there you have it. A few of the most important fundamentals of meaningful communication. Before you move on, however, we want to leave you with one more thing. We want to give you a quick way of pulling all these skills together and putting them into practice.

Not long ago, on a flight from Denver to Seattle, we found ourselves in the middle of a complete communication breakdown as we were trying to talk about laundry. Can you believe it? We were flying 35,000 feet above the planet and unable to have a coherent conversation about getting our laundry room under control. It started when we were thumbing through a magazine and saw a photo of a stackable washer and dryer depicted in a spotless laundry room.

"Why can't our laundry room look like that?" asked Les.

As the words fell from Les's lips, I felt my body stiffen. This wasn't the first time we'd covered this ground. Throughout our marriage we have tossed the chore of laundry back and forth. But recently it's been my responsibility, and with two little boys it was becoming more of a challenge.

"If you want to do the laundry now, be my guest," I said in a snippy tone while stuffing the magazine in the seat pocket.

With that, we were off and running. If you were eavesdropping from the seat behind us, you never would have known that we were on our way home from giving a marriage seminar to hundreds of couples. We admit it. We weren't even close to practicing what we preach. So we finally resorted to a strategy we developed for just such an occasion (we've been down this path more than once!).

When we get stuck in a communication meltdown, we get out our cheat sheet. It's a small card reminding us of the most important communication skills we know. It gets us back to the fundamentals, and it contains only one sentence: "Seek to understand before being understood."

That's it. This simple thought, popularized by Stephen Covey in his book *The Seven Habits of Highly Effective People,* changes our entire mindset and inevitably gets us back on track. We know it sounds simple, but it is profound. And it works. Once you reframe your predicament to try to understand your partner before you try to get him or her to understand you, your communication skills, no matter how rudimentary, take a quantum leap.

After a quick look at our cheat sheet, I

relaxed my defensive posture and worked to understand Les's perspective. "You really value having an organized and orderly life, and I sometimes forget how much that means to you." I could barely believe the words were coming out of my mouth. Les immediately recognized my sincerity and soon acknowledged the struggle to keep up with our growing family's requirements. Our entire conversation turned around. We began to practice what we preach and got back on track with a civilized and constructive conversation.

So take it from a couple of very human relationship experts. Next time you get stuck trying to put all these recommendations into practice, pull out a cheat sheet and remind yourself of this elementary point. Once you are seeking to understand before being understood, the rest of these skills fall much more naturally into place.

CHAPTER FOUR:
THE FOUNDATION OF EVERY
GREAT CONVERSATION
UNCOVERING YOUR FEAR FACTOR

Words came tumbling out of me like coins
from a change dispenser.
Natascha Wodin

Meet Dr. Myron R. Fox, the most impressive communicator you'll never understand. He leans on his lectern at the front of an auditorium where dozens of learned people have come to hear him speak. And all the while, Dr. Fox goes out of his way to be sure he makes absolutely no sense. The audience is riveted, nodding in agreement as he gibbers on with eloquent style and fluent finesse about nothing. His non sequiturs and contradictory statements are met with nods of agreement.

You've entered the twilight zone? Nope. Just a research experiment at the University of Pennsylvania. Professor Scott Armstrong is testing his "Dr. Fox Hypothesis," based on an actor posing as Dr. Myron R. Fox, who is patching together raw material from unrelated *Scientific American* articles combined with meaningless references to unconnected topics and a hefty dose of doubletalk. Armstrong wants to know if "an unintelligible communication from a legitimate source in the recipient's area of expertise will increase the recipient's rating of the author's competence." Turns out, it does. The scholarly audience of professionals reported on anonymous questionnaires that they "found the lecture clear and stimulating."[1]

Imagine that! You can say absolutely nothing of value and still be respected. Truth is, for couples, that's not as silly as it might seem. The very point of communication is to enjoy the comfort of an ongoing emotional connection even when your words are rather meaningless. It's what Charles Lamb was getting at when he said, " 'Tis the privilege of friendship to talk nonsense, and have her nonsense respected."

And it is a privilege. When you have a partnership that allows you both to talk unedited, to speak freely, you are enjoying one of the great privileges of a healthy relationship. It's an elite status among couples who feel safe enough to talk about whatever they think and feel.

There is no need to test the Dr. Fox

Hypothesis in your own relationship. When the two of you are shooting the breeze about anything and everything, meaningful or not, and still feeling connected deep in your soul, you are speaking Love Talk. And achieving Love Talk has everything to do with feeling safe. "Friendship is the inexpressible comfort of feeling safe with a person," said British author George Eliot, "having neither to weigh thoughts nor measure words." When it comes to conversation, we are all hardwired for emotional safety. Each of us has an overwhelming need to feel free from potential pain, loss, or danger. This compelling need is the driving force behind the way each of us lives our life. It is the prime motivator behind almost everything we do — especially when it comes to conversation.

In fact, once you find your safety zone as a couple, once you tap into exactly what makes you feel most protected, relaxed, and welcome, you can eliminate what we call your personal fear factor — whether you know it or not, it's your biggest roadblock to enjoying Love Talk.

Your Personal Fear Factor
Only rarely does someone (the most self-aware and insightful) say, "I feel unsafe, and

that's why I'm doing what I'm doing in my relationship," yet this fear of being at personal risk is lurking underneath nearly all of our conversations. When our fear of losing what we deeply value increases, so does our insecurity, and that's when our conversations get twisted. For this very reason, we want to help you identify your personal fear factor. We all have one. Each and every one of us has a fear of losing something we value in the daily exchanges of our relationship. We may fear losing time, approval, loyalty, or quality.

So allow us to pose a simple multiple-choice question that will help you uncover your fear factor. For you, to get any meaning out of this question, however, we want you to answer it from deep inside. Think it over. Be brutally honest with yourself. Don't answer with what you think sounds best. Answer with what you know is really true. Here's the question: *What makes you feel most emotionally safe?*

- gaining control of time
- winning approval from others
- maintaining loyalty
- achieving quality standards

If you had to choose one of these as your

top emotional safety need, which would it be? Instead of choosing just one, you may prefer to rank the list of safety needs from strongest to weakest. That's fine. The point is to identify what gives you the greatest sense of emotional security.

And if you are wondering why we are having you choose from among this specific list of safety needs, we have good reason. For nearly a century, these four fundamental needs have been consistently identified through research as the best predictors of human behavior and interaction.[2]

Talking much about oneself can also be a means to conceal oneself.
Friedrich Nietzsche

So which need tops your list? Once you identify it, we want to help you corroborate it. In a moment we will show you how an online instrument can verify your primary fear factor, and more important, how you can use this knowledge to improve your communication. Before we get to the online Love Talk Indicator, however, let's consider your instinctive answer to this question. See if these brief descriptions ring true for you.

Did you skip the prologue to this book? That's okay. We know how you feel. Urgent. Right? Do you live in fear of wasting your time? Do you feel that if you don't aggressively protect it, your time will soon be slipping away unproductively? Well, here's some news that probably won't brighten your day. In a lifetime, the average American will spend:

- six months sitting at stoplights
- eight months opening junk mail
- one year looking for misplaced objects
- two years unsuccessfully returning phone calls
- five years waiting in line[3]

Like we said, probably not the best news you've heard all day — especially if gaining control of your time is where and when you feel most emotionally secure. By the way, have you ever felt that a driver was really slow in pulling out of the parking space you were waiting for? It turns out your imagination may not be playing tricks on you. A recent study of 400 drivers in a shopping mall found that drivers took longer to pull out of a space if someone was waiting than if nobody was waiting there to claim the space. On average, if nobody was waiting for the space, drivers took 32.2 seconds to pull out of a spot after opening a car door. If someone was waiting, drivers took about 39 seconds. And woe to the person who honks to hurry a driver: drivers took 43 seconds to pull out of a space when the waiting driver honked![4]

So keep this in mind the next time you're roaming the lot for an open space — especially if gaining control of your time brings you comfort. We know that may not be easy. After all, "impatient" may be one of the ways your friends have come to describe you. You guard your time.

In fact, if you find your safety comes primarily from controlling your time, you'll tend to aggressively protect it. You aren't about to let these discouraging descriptions of time wasters describe your life. You're not going to allow five years of your life to be swiped by standing in lines. You don't mess around when you have a task to accomplish, and you sure don't want to waste even a minute on something you don't value. You're eager to get to the bottom line. You prize efficiency and you value brief communication, clear and to the point. You're a natural planner and you're results-oriented.

> There is no greater lie than
> a truth misunderstood.
> William James

NFL head coach Steve Mariucci says, "I never wear a watch, because I always know it's now — and now is when you should do it." Do you identify with this quip? Is Steve your kind of guy? If so, your top emotional safety need just might be gaining control of your time.

Winning Approval from Others

"Do you like me? Check yes or no." Remember this little ditty scrawled on a piece of notebook paper and folded up several times? It was to the little classmate you had a crush on in sixth grade. Pretty straightforward, don't you think? Not if this is your top emotional safety need. No matter how old you are, it's the question you have on your mind (at least unconsciously) most of the time.

If you find your safety in the approval of other people — especially those you deeply respect — you fear doing something or saying something that might offend or put them off. Your conversations around those you respect are energetic and optimistic, even inspirational. Facts and data take a temporary backseat to the emotion you put into your message.

The film *Gladiator* tells the story of Maximus, general of the Roman army in AD 180. Following victory in a decisive battle, the dying emperor Marcus Aurelius expresses his desire to appoint Maximus as his successor. Marcus Aurelius's own son, Commodus, is the amoral opposite of Maximus. When Commodus learns he will not be the next emperor, he recoils from his father.

"You wrote to me once, listing the four chief virtues: wisdom, justice, fortitude, and temperance," says Commodus. "As I read the list, I knew I had none of them. But I have other virtues: ambition — that can be a virtue when it drives us to excel; resourcefulness; courage — perhaps not on the battlefield, but there are many forms of courage; devotion — to my family, to you. But none of my virtues were on your list. Even then it was as if you did not want me for your son."

"Commodus, you go too far," replies his father, the emperor.

Commodus continues: "I searched the faces of the gods for ways to please you, to make you proud. One kind word, one full hug where you pressed me to your chest and held me tight would have been like the sun in my heart for a thousand years. All I've ever wanted was to live up to you, Caesar, Father."

> Love takes off masks that we fear we cannot live without and know we cannot live within.
> James Baldwin

Does this scene tug at your heart? Do you resonate with his desire? Do you feel his hunger for a full hug that would be like the sun in your heart for a thousand years? You do if winning the approval of those you respect is your top emotional safety need. How could you not? The approval and blessing from a father to his child is major. We all want it and need it. But the person with this safety need extends it vigorously to most other relationships, especially if they didn't get it growing up.

Maintaining Loyalty
When Pepper Rodgers' football players at UCLA were having difficulty adapting to the wishbone offense he'd installed and the school's alumni demanded that he adopt

another system, Rodgers didn't budge. The wishbone, he said, "is like Christianity. If you believe in it only until something goes wrong, you didn't believe in it in the first place." Rodgers was loyal to his system. He joked that nobody in Southern California would hang out with him during that time. "My dog was my only true friend," Rodgers said of that year. "I told my wife that every man needs at least two good friends. She bought me another dog."

If your safety needs are met primarily through commitment and the stability of what is known, you understand Pepper Rodgers. You also fear change — at least the kind of change that happens without warning and threatens your fundamental loyalties. You value devotion. You prefer predictability and instinctually resist change unless it occurs at a slow and steady pace. You're a patient listener in conversations and a strong connection makes you feel secure.

Consider the loyalty and devotion between Frederic Douglass, who was born into slavery in Maryland in the early nineteenth century, and his mother. He writes in *Narrative of the Life of Frederick Douglass, an American Slave:* "My mother and I were separated when I was but an infant — before I knew her as my mother. She was hired by a Mr. Stewart, who lived about 12 miles from my home."

Nonetheless, young Frederick's mother found ways to see her son: "She made her journeys to see me in the night, traveling the whole distance on foot, after the performance of her day's work. She was a field hand, and a whipping was the penalty of not being in the field at sunrise." He continues: "She was with me in the night. She would lie down with me and get me to sleep, but long before I waked she was gone."

Frederick Douglass's mother, after working all day in the scorching heat and then walking 12 miles in the dark to see her son, would comfort him until he fell asleep. Then she'd walk another 12 miles back to avoid getting whipped.

Talk about loyalty, devotion, and commitment. Thankfully, these qualities will not be put to this kind of test for most of us, but if loyalty is your top security need, you would probably pass the test. Are you resistant to change? Do you prize the idea of being there for the person who needs you, and does this kind of dependability and reliability from your partner make you feel safe?

> Talk to a man about himself and he will listen for hours.
> Benjamin Disraeli

Achieving Quality Standards

Known for its luxury watches, Swiss watchmaker Patek Philippe has also become well known for its clever advertising slogan: "You never actually own a Patek Philippe; you merely take care of it for the next generation." If you resonate with this sentiment, you probably have your basic emotional safety need met in achieving quality standards. You like the idea that, like a fine timepiece, your character can be crafted and maintained through a series of good decisions.

In fact, if your safety needs are met primarily through maintaining a high standard and impeccable reputation, you fear making a choice that would tarnish it. You approach decisions with a great deal of thought. You know there is a right way and a wrong way of doing things, and you're determined to find the right way, no matter how much time it takes. You're conservative and cautious in your conversations, never promising more than you can deliver.

Unhappy fans voiced their displeasure when Scott Hoch refused to hit his nine-foot birdie putt on the second play-off hole of the 2003 Ford Championship at Doral in Miami, Florida. As darkness fell, Hoch was unsure about the lay of the green. So the tournament's sudden-death finish was delayed until the next morning, when many fans could not attend. Hoch sank his putt the next morning and then birdied a third play-off hole to win $900,000. Had Hoch tried to finish the tournament on Sunday, he probably would have lost. In the dwindling light, Hoch, who has had five eye operations, thought the putt would move left. His caddie saw it the other direction. The morning light proved the caddie right.

Hoch was not concerned about winning the approval of fans and felt no pressure by the clock. What mattered to Scott Hoch was making the best decision he could. And he took great care and caution to do so. Are you like that? Does achieving a quality standard rank higher than controlling your time, winning approval, and maintaining loyalty? If so, quality is your emotional safety need.

Building Your Safety Zone

Maybe you saw the movie *Panic Room* in which Jodie Foster plays a woman who is frightened by burglars who have broken into her New York City condo. She retreats with her daughter to a high-tech "panic room" within her residence, a secret room with reinforced doors and other safety precautions. And if you're like us, that was the first time you'd ever heard of such a thing. Panic rooms, however, are not just in the movies. Apparently security companies regularly install what they refer to as "safe rooms." Most requests come from wealthy families or celebrities who fear being targets of harm. It is estimated there are thousands of such rooms in Bel Air and Beverly Hills alone.[5]

This got us to thinking about a "safe room" for our relationship, a place where we feel completely protected and secure. Can you imagine if your home had such a thing? You and your partner could enter this room and be free from the fear of losing time, approval, loyalty, and quality. Your deepest emotional fear would no longer be a factor in your conversations. You'd be safe. You could relax. And can you imagine the conversations you'd have there? They'd be the best conversations you ever had — ever dreamed of having. Before long, you'd find you were spending nearly all your time in your safe room.

You get the idea. Once you — each of you — identify your primary fear factor, you can build your own emotional safe room, free from the fear of losing what you value most. Sound too good to be true? It's not. We are about to hand you the tools you need to get started on creating a relational safety zone — a space in your relationship that is tailored precisely to the combination of your two fear factors. How can we do this? By having you consider four eye-opening questions that are critically important to Love Talk. You'll be glad to know, by the way, there are no right or wrong answers to these questions. They are designed to help you understand yourself, your partner, and your relationship. They will reveal your personal talk style — showing you how you uniquely say the things you do.

> If virtue precede us
> every step will be safe.
>
> Seneca

Your Talk Style

Let's get straight to it. Each of you has a unique talk style. So unique that we can almost guarantee your two talk styles are not alike. In fact, they may be polar opposites in some ways. But we're getting ahead of ourselves. Your unique talk styles are determined by how you individually answer these four questions:

- How do you tackle problems?
- How do you influence each other?
- How do you react to change?
- How do you make decisions?

Your answer to each of these questions pinpoints a specific dimension of communication that has been proven to be paramount in understanding how you say the things you do and how you hear what your partner is saying. In other words, once you accurately understand how you tackle problems, influence your partner, react to change, and make decisions, you will know your talk style — and this knowledge is the key to enjoying Love Talk. So let's explore each one.

■ ■ ■ ■

PART 2
How You Say the
Things You Do

■ ■ ■ ■

How you answer the next four questions uncovers your personal talk style. And accurately understanding your talk style is the key to unlocking Love Talk. Not until both of you know your own style as well as each other's can you rest in the safety of a conversation in which fear is no longer a factor — a conversation in which you are no longer burdened by having to weigh thoughts or measure words.

CHAPTER FIVE:
HOW DO YOU TACKLE PROBLEMS?

AGGRESSIVELY OR PASSIVELY

If the only tool you have is a hammer,
you tend to see every problem as a nail.
Abraham Maslow

"Do I smell hairspray?" I asked.

"No," Leslie responded.

"You don't smell anything?" I asked with more urgency. I had just woken up and wandered into the kitchen for a glass of juice.

"It's probably the Brilliant Shine I just used by the entryway mirror."

"Brilliant Shine?!"

"Yeah, it makes my hair shiny," Leslie said.

"I don't care what it does; it stinks. Open the front door and let's get some fresh air in here."

Leslie opened the door for a couple of seconds, literally. She closed the door abruptly to keep our toddler from escaping.

"I'll open this window," she said as she lifted it up about two inches.

"That's not going to do it," I said as I opened the French doors to our back deck and made a beeline to open the front door she had just closed. "Is that necessary?" Leslie asked as I whisked by her to turn on the ventilation fan above the stove.

It was to me. The unpleasant smell of her hair product was a repulsive way to start my day, and I wanted it gone. Now.

"The odor will take care of itself if you just give it some time," said Leslie.

The Aggressive Problem Solver's Safety Need Is Time

Time. That was the issue. Brilliant Shine was wasting my time — and I prize my time. In fact, my biggest fear factor is losing my time. So guess what? That makes me an aggressive problem solver. I admit it. And after two decades of marriage, Leslie knows it as well as I do. I don't mess around. When it comes to solving problems, I take the proverbial bull by the horns. I'm not afraid of confrontation. I want to get to the bottom of any issue in the most direct path possible.

Leslie, on the other hand, tends to be a passive problem solver. Notice how she just wanted the problem of the smelly hair product to take care of itself. And that's just fine — if losing control of your time isn't your primary fear factor. And for Leslie, it isn't. So she approaches problem solving from a completely different angle. When faced with a problem, she's more accommodating than assertive. More docile than decisive. More passive than aggressive. For her, problem solving is a gentle sport because gaining control of her time is her lowest emotional safety need — by a long shot. And she's far more patient when it comes to solving problems than I am.

So do our different approaches to problem solving impact our relationship? Do they interfere with our communication? Only on a daily basis! It's the greatest source of miscommunication we have.

It can't help but be an issue for us. Anyone with an aggressive approach to problem solving asks direct questions and demands answers, often without feeling the need for tact or diplomacy. *Let's get the problem solved, then we can be nice to each other* is the attitude of the aggressive problem solver. They are task-oriented. And when something begins to threaten their time, they become hard-driving, assertive, and bold. And when that problem is not quickly solved or when they feel their partner isn't lending a hand with the same sense of urgency, they become more blunt, strong-willed, and impatient. Take it from Leslie, an aggressive problem solver is no fun to be around when his problems aren't getting solved.

The Passive Problem Solver

Bill and Ed had the tiring job of clearing a field of trees. The contract called for them to be paid per tree. Bill wanted the day to be profitable, so he grunted and sweated, swinging the axe relentlessly.

Ed, on the other hand, seemed to be working about half as fast. He even took a rest and sat off to the side for a few minutes. Bill kept chopping away until every muscle and tendon in his body was screaming.

At the end of the day, Bill was terribly sore, but Ed was smiling and telling jokes. Amazingly, Ed had cut down more trees. Bill said, "I noticed you sitting while I worked without a break. How'd you out-work me?"

> No problem is so formidable that
> you can't walk away from it.
> Charles M. Schulz

Ed smiled. "Did you notice I was sharpening my axe while I was sitting?"

Sometimes the seemingly more passive, less hurried approach to problem solving is the smarter tactic. The gung-ho problem solver, so eager to achieve results, can overlook what the passive problem solver is likely to see. People who are passive — who don't have the loss of time as one of their primary emotional security needs — are a great asset to problem solving. By nature they are cautious. They want to gather information and study the problem before jumping into solving it. Bottom line, the passive problem solver is willing to give it time.

Of course, this is the one gift an aggressive problem solver doesn't want to give. Asking them to give up time, to slow down the process, is like asking a race car driver at the Indy 500 to relax and just take it easy for a few laps. It's not going to happen.

And that's exactly why a passive problem solver can be a good compliment to an aggressive one.

Bill and Cindy had a problem. Weeds. And lots of them. "The neighbors are starting to talk about our yard," said Bill. "And Kenny promised to take care of this when we talked last week — I'm calling his parents to get him over here right now."

"Honey, put the phone down," said Cindy. "Kenny is just a high schooler who cuts our grass. He's not a professional gardener. There's no need to call his parents."

"Well, this is embarrassing. I'll do it myself."

Cindy laughed out loud. "Bill, I've never seen you do any yard work. Are you sure about this? I'm sure Kenny has his reasons, and he said he'd be here tomorrow."

Bill rolled his eyes and headed off to buy some weed killer. "I'll be back in a few minutes, and those weeds will be toast before the sun goes down."

Sure enough. Within the hour, Bill was squirting his fast-acting weed killer on every weed he could find in his front yard.

"You've been working hard out there," said Cindy as Bill reentered the house.

"There's really nothing to it. I just don't understand why Kenny said he couldn't do it himself today. That really makes me mad to be spending my day off doing his job."

"Well, I know you're irritated, but you solved your problem."

At least he thought he'd solved his problem. The next day, Kenny pulled up to their home and rang the doorbell. "What happened to your lawn?" he asked Cindy.

"Oh my goodness!" Cindy shouted. "Bill,

you'd better see this."

He came to the front door as the three of them surveyed a yard that looked like a giant slice of Swiss cheese. There were dozens of huge holes in the grass. Big brown circles in what would have otherwise been a lovely lawn.

"You didn't use this stuff, did you, Mr. Brown?" Kenny asked Bill as he pointed to the empty bottle of weed killer. "I didn't want to work on your weeds yesterday because the wind was so strong and that spreads the spray. Plus, I wouldn't recommend this brand of weed killer. It says right here, 'Important: Not recommended for spot weed control in lawns because it kills grasses.' You didn't do that, did you, Mr. Brown?"

With that, Cindy retreated into the house, leaving Bill to explain his aggressive problem-solving strategy to their teenage gardener.

Like we said, sometimes a passive approach that waits for the solution to emerge in time is the smarter way to go. Of course, there's a downside to being a passive problem solver as well. Namely, time doesn't always lead to solutions. If an aggressive approach isn't eventually taken, life becomes a jumble of loose ends that never get tied up.

Mixing Passive and Aggressive Approaches to Problem Solving

The passive problem solver's relaxed approach can obviously exacerbate an aggressive partner (not that we need a scientific study to demonstrate this fact in our own marriage!). After all, the passive problem solver is far more careful and considerate, wanting to avoid conflict and steer clear of any tension. This approach comes off as unmotivated and indecisive to an aggressive partner. You get the picture. And so does any passive problem solver who has been on the receiving end of a forceful problem solver.

It's true. I (Leslie) can't count the number of times I've gotten my feelings hurt because I didn't understand Les's aggressive approach. The problem could be a lost cell phone, a dirty laundry room, a spilled bowl of Cheerios, or finding a babysitter, a good restaurant, or a misplaced TV remote. The problem doesn't matter. It's the infringement of his time and the overwhelming urgency that matters. *Why is he so sharp with me?* I often wondered in these situations. *Doesn't he know this hurts my feelings?* Truth is, he didn't know he was hurting my feelings, not at first. He was bewildered by my low-key approach to finding the lost cell phone or whatever. He simply couldn't fathom that I would not be as goal-oriented as he to solve the problem.

> I don't have any solution but I certainly admire the problem.
> Ashleigh Brilliant

Not until I understood Les's primary fear factor as being the loss of time did I get a clue to his aggressive problem solving. That's when it clicked. That's when I began to attain not only a new understanding of it, but a more compassionate and graceful spirit to cope with it. In fact, this single insight has bolstered my ability to be more objective and take things like this less personally. After all, his determined and direct approach to problem solving is about him, not me.

> There is no human problem which could not be solved if people would simply do as I advise.
> Gore Vidal

And not until Les learned that losing control of my time is of little consequence to me (compared to other safety needs) did he begin to understand my passive approach. He is now far less likely to read apathy into my mild-mannered problem solving. He and I both know we are hardwired differently on this continuum, and this understanding gives us both more grace and takes us one step closer to Love Talk.

Aggressive Problem Solver

Says: "Let's do it now."
Strengths: Self-starter, bold, determined, and tenacious
Under stress becomes: Impatient and blunt
In conflict becomes: Intimidating and confrontational

Passive Problem Solver

Says: "Let's give it some time."
Strengths: Considerate, self-controlled, patient, and cooperative
Under stress becomes: Anxious and slow
In conflict becomes: Indecisive and withdrawn

Curious to know where you and your partner come down on this problem-solving issue? You may have a pretty good idea already. Maybe like us you are each in different camps. Or perhaps you are both aggressive problem solvers or both passive problem solvers. Whatever your combination, we have some specific help for you. Before we leave you in Part Two of this book, we will provide you with a unique and powerful way of knowing exactly where both of you land. We'll help you precisely pinpoint how aggressively or passively each of you approaches problem solving and give you a few personalized ways for maximizing your combination of styles. At this stage we simply want to help you reflect on the four questions that determine your talk styles, so let's move to the next question.

CHAPTER SIX:
HOW DO YOU INFLUENCE EACH OTHER?

WITH FEELINGS OR FACTS

Freedom is that instant between when someone tells you to do something and when you decide how to respond.
Jeffrey Borenstein

Humorist Mark Twain influenced the American literary landscape perhaps more than any other author. He changed the way we think and feel about national landmarks like the Mississippi River. He's also one of the most quoted authors of all time, still selling millions of books a century after his death. Few would dispute his enduring influence.

The dramatic influence Twain had on his wife was just as powerful but not nearly as well known. He was not a religious man, nor did he claim to be when he began courting Olivia Langdon. Back in Twain's day, a man typically had to get permission from a woman's parents before marrying her. Mark Twain had a problem, however. Olivia's

Christian parents would not allow their daughter to marry an unbeliever. To overcome this obstacle, Twain took on the guise of a spiritual seeker who needed the support and prayers of Olivia's family.

Twain, seemingly influenced by Olivia's prodding, presumably converted. He wrote to his mother after his engagement to Olivia: "My prophecy was correct . . . Olivia said she never could or would love me — but she set herself the task of making a Christian of me. I said she would succeed, but that in the meantime she would unwittingly dig a matrimonial pit and end by tumbling in it — and lo! the prophecy is fulfilled."

Olivia's family was convinced Twain was a Christian and permitted the marriage. But at least one scholar insists that Twain "was a man in love, wooing a woman he hoped to marry. His 'religious' feelings at that time, expressed in love letters to Olivia, disappeared as soon as the nuptials were over."[1]

After their wedding, Twain ridiculed Olivia's beliefs. Soon Olivia's optimism began to wane, and her fervent faith cooled. Eventually she forsook her religion altogether, and a deep sorrow deluged Olivia's life. Mark Twain loved her and never meant to hurt her, but he had broken her spirit. He said, "Livy, if it comforts you to lean on your faith, do so."

She replied sadly, "I cannot. I do not have any faith left." Twain often wished he could restore Olivia's faith, hope, and optimism, but it was too late.[2]

> Trust your hunches. They're usually based on facts filed away just below the conscious level.
> Joyce Brothers

The influence one person can have on another is difficult to exaggerate. Given enough time, a spouse can drill down to the very core of a partner's spirit and influence the things she holds most dearly. Of course, few of us succumb to the kinds of crafty measures Mark Twain employed, but we are just as susceptible as Olivia if we underestimate the import of influence we have on each other.

Every day in nearly every way we are attempting to influence one another. Our conversations are consumed by it: "You're not going to wear that, are you?" "How can you support a candidate who has this kind of a record?" "Did you know that men who don't have a physical checkup at your age are twice as likely to have a medical problem within the next five years?" "I know you don't like lemons, but you're going to love this lemon cake — I just know it."

Our attempts to influence each other, on the mundane as well as the major issues of life, are unending. Influencing each other to do this or that or not to do something at all involves an untold portion of your daily conversations. And knowing whether your spouse is influenced more powerfully by feelings or by facts can go a long way in making your conversations more productive.

Facts or Feelings?

"My cell phone may break up," said Steve. "I just need you to know that it looks like this meeting is going to end early — can you pick me up?"

"Okay, I think I will take I-90," said Patti. "Linda told me about these new lights in the tunnel. I guess they're really cool — like space-age or something."

"I just checked the traffic report on my laptop five minutes ago, and I-90 is backed up, so the 202 is definitely the way to get here."

"That's sweet, babe, but I never have

problems on I-90, so don't worry about it."

"What?" asks Steve. "I just told you you've got to take the 202 or you'll run into traffic. Are you listening? Patti, just get here as soon as you can. I don't want to be waiting around after this meeting ends. I'm eager to get home, so take the 202. It has less traffic, plus they're doing road construction on I-90. The facts speak for themselves."

"Oh, remind me to tell you about my conversation with Tina today. You're going to love this one."

"Patti, we can talk about all that when you get here. Just get here as soon as you can and take the 202!"

"Stevie, I'm leaving right now — I love you."

Here's a couple at opposite ends of the Influence Scale. Steve influences with facts while Patti is all about feelings. "Facts, schmacks" is her attitude. She's animated rather than analytical. She's optimistic rather than objective. Patti is fun-loving, the life of the party. Her fear factor? Losing the approval of others — especially Steve.

But, unwittingly, that's exactly what she does in this instance.

"Hey, babe, have you been waiting long?" Patti asks as she pulls up to the curb where Steve is standing with his briefcase in hand.

"You have to see the new lights in the tunnel — they are amazing!"

Steve grunts as he climbs into the car.

"How was the meeting?"

"Fine," Steve sighs.

"I got you a double-shot latte. It's there in the cup holder."

Steve sits silent, eyes on the road.

"So you won't believe what Tina told me this morning," Patti says. She takes a sip from her coffee and waits for a response from Steve. There is none. "Do you want to hear about it?" Patti asks.

"Not really."

"Stevie, what's wrong?"

"You know what's wrong."

And so do you. Steve laid out the facts to Patti as plain as day. He wanted her to take the fastest route and not leave him stranded. He's a critical thinker, not swayed by emotion. He's analytical and rational. He doesn't care if the lights in the tunnel are great or if he's going to get a cup of coffee. That's irrelevant to the fact that he wanted to be picked up on time and that Patti needed to take the 202 in order to do so. And because she didn't, he feels as though Patti doesn't listen to him or care about the reality of the issue.

"I asked you to take the 202 so you

wouldn't be late," Steve continues. "Instead, you stopped to get coffee and took I-90. I don't get it."

"Honey, I know you often enjoy a latte after a meeting like that, so I thought I'd bring you one. I thought you'd be happy about it."

> Facts are stubborn things; and whatever may be our wishes, our inclinations, or the dictates of our passions, they cannot alter the state of facts and evidence.
> John Quincy Adams

"All I wanted to do was get home. I told you that and I told you how to do it, but you just ignored it. You just don't listen. Or maybe it's that you just don't care. Is that it?"

There's a long pause in the tension-filled car.

"Patti, you do this to me all the time. I give you the facts and you act as though you didn't even hear me. Now I've missed the first two innings of the Mariners game."

Patti is struck by a thud in her gut. She's let Steve down and instantly feels like she has lost his approval or trust. By default, she feels unsafe. She's losing what she wants most — Steve's appreciation and approval for bringing him a latte. This translates into a quantum leap in anxiety for Patti, and she starts to tear up.

"Why are you crying?" Steve asks.

Patti dabs the corners of her eyes with a tissue.

"I'm not mad at you," says Steve. "I just don't understand why this happens."

If Your Fear Factor Is Approval, You'll Influence with Feelings

Ever been there? Ever felt like your partner's approval was slipping through your hands? If so, you probably influence him or her with feelings rather than facts. And you yourself are influenced more by feelings than facts. You want to have fun and you aren't about to let facts stand in your way. And, as for Patti, the facts may not even register for you on occasion. You aren't tuned into the objective data as much as you are the emotional sway of the moment. For example, you can imagine a positive interaction (like taking a latte to your partner) and begin to concoct it without measuring it against the objective facts (such as his primary desire for you to be on time). Of course, this misreading of the facts can come through to your partner as being inattentive and unreliable. And given enough time, this begins to create distrust. In other words, the very thing you long for, the thing that makes you feel most safe — winning your partner's approval — becomes illusive because your optimistic and effervescent approach leads you to miss what it is that your partner desires.

Steve, on the other hand, doesn't have winning approval as one of his top safety needs. And because of this, he brings rational insight and critical thinking into every conversation. He's not likely to be swayed by a warm, fuzzy feeling as much as he is by cold hard facts. As a result, he can be quite critical and cool. He'll ask the tough questions when everyone else is riding high on emotion. He'll invite skepticism to replace enthusiasm. That's why he begins to lose trust in Patti when she doesn't rely on black-and-white facts the way he does. But then again, that's also why Patti infuses his life with the fun of full color.

Are Patti and Steve doomed to crisscrossed communication? Absolutely not. They have huge potential to make a great team in this area once they both understand each other's style. In fact, this understanding will cause them to see how invaluable

> It is more fun to talk with someone who doesn't use long, difficult words but rather short, easy words like "What about lunch?"
> Pooh's Little Instruction Book

they are to each other. Patti needs Steve's logical questions, and Steve needs Patti's fun-loving perspective.

Now consider this same conversation topic between Ken and Judy, who are both more apt to influence each other with facts than with feelings.

"My cell phone may break up," says Ken. "I need you to pick me up sooner than I thought, so take the 202 and it will save you ten minutes this time of day."

"Are you sure? Have you checked the traffic report?"

"Yes, the 202 is your best bet."

"Did you check the report recently?"

"Just five minutes ago."

"Okay, I think you're right. Plus there's road construction on I–90."

"Right. That could be a real mess."

"I'm leaving right now, hon."

See the difference? Who wouldn't? It's hard to not notice the disparity between

Patti's creative negotiating approach and Judy's calm and logical approach. All the facts may line up, but if it doesn't feel right to a person whose safety need is winning approval from others, they set the facts aside. And since they are optimistic by nature, they influence with inspiration rather than introspection.

Does this make them a better match? Yes and no. Sure, they may have fewer arguments than Steve and Patti when it comes to how they influence each other, but they are bound to be quite opposite on one of the other dimensions, such as how they tackle problems. It's a fact. No couple is going to be perfectly matched on how they tackle problems, influence each other, and all the other dimensions we are about to explore. So Steve and Patti's conversation may seem dreadful in comparison to Ken and Judy's, but that's only because we are isolating one example of how they influence each other.

In case you're curious, Les and I are both prone to influencing each other with feelings more than facts. We persuade each other more with enthusiasm and encouragement than we do with logic. We don't neglect rational input or logical influence altogether, but because we both find emotional safety in winning each other's approval, feelings win out over facts almost every time. It's just the way we are.

You're Hardwired for Facts or Feelings

Let's clear something up just in case it's roaming around in your head. People don't choose to be influenced by facts or by feelings, just as they don't choose how short or how tall they are. How we are influenced is part of our makeup. While we do have a say in how we will influence our partner, we can't do much about what influences us on this continuum.

Take a lesson from George Banks, played by Steve Martin, in the comedy film *Father of the Bride.* As George narrates the story, we learn of his anxiety surrounding the preparations for and the huge expense of his daughter's wedding. Always aware of the large sum of money he's spending, George teeters on the brink of maniacal rage. When he finds out that the reception will cost $250 a head, George finally hits the roof. On an errand for his wife, George stands in a supermarket aisle and tears open a bag of hot-dog buns. A stock boy looks on in wonder and politely asks, "Excuse me, sir. What are you doing?"

> To be persuasive, we must be believable. To be believable, we must be credible. To be credible, we must be truthful.
>
> Edward R. Murrow

George shouts, "I'll tell you what I'm doing! I want to buy eight hot dogs and eight hot-dog buns to go with them. But no one sells eight hot-dog buns. They only sell twelve hot-dog buns! So I end up paying for four buns I don't need! So I am removing the superfluous buns!"

"I'm sorry, sir," says the boy calmly, "but you're gonna have to pay for all twelve buns. They're not marked individually."

George says, "Yeah, you know why? Because some big shot over at the wiener company got together with some big shot over at the bun company and decided to rip off the American public because they think the American public is a bunch of trusting nitwits who'll pay for things they don't need rather than making a stink! Well, they're not ripping off this nitwit anymore, because I'm not paying for one more thing I don't need! GEORGE BANKS IS SAYING NO!"

Later, when George's daughter, Annie, calls the wedding off, he tries to console his future son-in-law, explaining that Annie inherited his tendency to blow up over small things. George explains, "Annie comes from a long line of major overreactors. . . . Me, I can definitely lose it. My mother . . . a nut. My grandfather . . . stories about him were legendary."

Suddenly, George has an epiphany: "That's when it hit me: Annie was just like me."

And chances are your hardwiring for being influenced more by facts or more by feelings was passed down from your family. It's in your hardwiring. And that's exactly why understanding your partner's hardwiring on this dimension is vital to improving your communication.

Influence by Feelings

Says: "Trust me, it will work great."
Strengths: Optimistic, friendly, outgoing, and inspiring
Under stress becomes: Impulsive and unrealistic
In conflict becomes: Poor listener and unreliable

Says: "Let's look at all the evidence."
Strengths: Realistic, logical, reflective, and calm
Under stress becomes: Pessimistic and introspective
In conflict becomes: Skeptical and uncommunicative

What about you and your partner? Again, you may already have a pretty good idea where you each stand, but we're going to show you precisely in just a few moments. We're also going to give you dozens of practical ways to improve your conversations once you accurately understand how each of you tends to be influenced most. Next, however, we turn to the third important question for cracking the code of your talk style and achieving Love Talk.

CHAPTER SEVEN:
HOW DO YOU
REACT TO CHANGE?
WITH RESISTANCE OR ACCEPTANCE

God grant me the serenity to accept the
things I cannot change, the courage to
change the things I can, and the wisdom
to know the difference.

Reinhold Neibuhr

"I've got to pick up some baby formula at
the grocery before we go home," I said to
Les as we were driving.

"Okay, I need to stop by the office and
get my mail anyway," he responded.

"Why don't you do that after you drop
the boys and me off at the house? Jack is
starving."

"It will only take a second — hey," Les
interrupted himself and pointed across the
street. "There's that new grocery that was
written up in the paper yesterday."

"What are you doing?" I asked as Les
changed lanes and started to take an unexpected turn.

"I'm going back to that store." He said

this with ramped-up energy and excitement in his voice. "I've got to do a U-turn."

"No, no. I want to go to Safeway by our house," I protested.

"Why? This will be fun. They're supposed to have a guy playing the piano in there while you shop, and I bet they're giving out free samples of food. The kids will love it, and I want to see what all the buzz is about."

"Please, no. This isn't the time. I need to go to Safeway where I know just where everything is."

"C'mon, you'll like it," Les said as he pulled into the parking lot.

"Safeway is better. I know the workers there and I wanted to say hi to Teresa."

"What?"

"I think her birthday is this week," I replied.

"You're kidding me, right? You know when the cashier's birthday is?"

"She's always so helpful to me. Seriously, I'd rather stop by Safeway. This place looks like a zoo."

"Okay, let me take a quick run through with John since we're here, and then we'll stop by Safeway."

Les climbs out of the car with our excited six-year-old and hustles across the parking lot, waving at me as I wait with our baby in the car.

That's me. Take it from Les, I'm not always the most accepting of change. I find comfort in the familiar. I have my habits. My routines. When it comes to change, I'm more resistant than accepting. More predictable than progressive. Les, on the other hand, is on the lookout to seize a new opportunity. And if one comes by, he'll change directions on a dime.

"We may need to fly to Phoenix next week," he could announce without warning. One phone call could change all his plans. And if the opportunity is a good one, he's fine with that. "Mike just called," he may say, "and he wants us to meet with his team down there — isn't that great?"

Of course, this news throws me for a complete loop — no matter how great the opportunity. *What about our boys?* I think. *Does this mean I'll miss my small group? I've scheduled a lunch with Tami next week. And I was looking forward to our date night.* While his first impulse to change is acceptance, my first impulse is resistance.

How you and your partner react to change makes a huge impact on your conversation. Whether you know it or not, much of your daily conversation centers on change. Contending with a calendar is a prime example. Think of all the conversations you have with each other about how you spend and don't spend your time. Will you keep your date on Thursday night now that a deadline has been bumped up at work? Will you change the time of your beach outing now that rain is predicted in the afternoon? Beyond your calendar, change consumes your conversations when you negotiate things like whether to go to your "usual" restaurant or something different, whether to buy a new car, whether to renew a magazine subscription, whether to rearrange your furniture, whether to change long-distance phone companies, and so on.

> Any change, even a change for the better, is always accompanied by drawbacks and discomforts.
> Arnold Bennett

Negotiating change is one of the four big conversational topics every couple encounters. And for this reason, it is imperative that you consider whether either one or both of you prize loyalty as one of your top emotional safety needs. For once you understand how each of you reacts to change, a big portion of your conversations will go much more smoothly.

If Your Safety Need Is Loyalty, You'll Be Resistant to Change

A few years ago, the Bayer Corporation stopped putting cotton in the top of their Genuine Bayer bottles of aspirin. The company realized the aspirin would hold up fine without the maddening white clumps, which it had included since 1914. "We concluded there really wasn't any reason to keep the cotton except tradition," said Chris Allen, Bayer's vice president of technical operations. "And despite the fact that it wasn't needed and that it actually made it more difficult to get to the aspirin, we still get complaints because some people don't like change."

I know exactly what he means. I (Leslie) tend to resist change. I prefer the slow and steady. I don't really care about cotton in my bottle of aspirin, but I do love tradition. Why? It goes back to one of my big fear factors — losing the stability that comes through loyalty. I'm loyal to my friends, to my colleagues, to my church, and to my husband. Loyal consistency makes me feel safe and secure. For me, friendships are for life. I don't just sign up to test out the relationship. If I'm your friend, you get me for the long haul whether you like it or not. And this deep safety need translates into loyalty in almost every area — even the grocery where I shop. Seems silly, I'm sure, if you don't have this need; but if you do, you know just what I mean.

Of course, my loyalty combined with my high need for approval (and thus my inclination to be influenced by feelings) makes me more prone to eventually come around to trying out a new grocery store or even catching an unexpected flight to Phoenix. After all, I'm loyal to Les, and if he wants to seize an opportunity, I'm likely to back him up. Eventually. Still, at my core, I'm resistant to change while he thrives on it.

The downside to resisting change is illustrated powerfully by James Belasco in his book *Teaching the Elephant to Dance.* He describes how trainers shackle young elephants with heavy chains to deeply embedded stakes, which is how they learn to stay in place. Older, powerful elephants never try to leave — even though they have the strength to pull the stake and walk away. Their conditioning has limited their movements. With only a small metal bracelet around their foot, they stand in place.

> None of us knows what the next change is going to be, what unexpected opportunity is just around the corner, waiting a few months or a few years to change all the tenor of our lives.
>
> Kathleen Norris

Like powerful elephants, we are sometimes bound by previously conditioned restraints. The statement "We have always done it this way" can be as limiting to a couple's progress as the unattached chain around an elephant's foot. After all, sometimes change is necessary. It's healthy. A promotion or a new job requires change. As does a chance for your child to excel by going to a different school. Progress mandates change. To let a good opportunity pass you by will burn to ashes all potential for realizing a dream. Just as the person who is accepting of change can get burned by an opportunity that never materializes, so can the person who is resistant to change become paralyzed by indecision.

Sometimes a rocky relationship comes to a stalemate because of one partner's resistance to change. "If you don't go with me to see a counselor, I'm out of here." That's when the couple enters a scary space, when the resistant person's deep need for loyalty is threatened to its very core — when they feel they may lose their partner's loyalty and commitment altogether. Even the conditioned elephant will change at this point. When the circus tent catches on fire and the elephant sees the flames and smells the smoke, it forgets its old conditioning and runs for its life.[1]

There's no need for any couple to get to this point. Even when one partner's top fear factor is losing loyalty, you can learn the principles of Love Talk to navigate even the toughest of terrain. We're going to show you how in chapter 9.

The One Change That's Always Welcome

No matter how resistant to change a person might be, one specific kind of change is always welcome. It's the kind of change that leads to loyalty. Rather than threatening a person's emotional security need, this kind of change actually bolsters it.

Consider Melvin Udall, the crude, obsessive-compulsive author played by Jack Nicholson in the film *As Good as It Gets*. Melvin offends everyone he meets. For example, the movie opens with him tossing a neighbor's pet down the laundry chute of the exclusive apartment building where he lives.

But Melvin becomes enamored with Carol Connelly, a waitress played by Helen Hunt. She has seen him at his worst but reluctantly agrees to meet Melvin at a fancy restaurant for a date. Carol arrives at the restaurant and is obviously ill at ease as waiters follow her about and wait on her hand and foot. While the other patrons of the restaurant are impeccably dressed, Carol wears a simple red dress.

Melvin sees Carol and waves her over to his table. When she approaches, Melvin hits an all-time low. "This restaurant!" he exclaims. "They make me buy a new outfit and let you in wearing a housedress." Carol is stunned and hurt. Yet she doesn't leave.

Instead, she looks Melvin in the eye and says, "Pay me a compliment, Melvin. I need one now."

Melvin responds, "I've got a great compliment." What could he possibly say to undo the thoughtless comment he had just delivered? He then gives one of the most romantic lines in big-screen history. This deeply flawed man, his own worst enemy, looks at Carol with all the kindness and sincerity his shriveled heart can muster and says, "Carol, you make me want to be a better man."

Now that's the kind of change all of us welcome — whether we are cautious or spontaneous. Changing one's ways to become a better person overrides even the strongest resistance to change because it brings about devotion and cultivates commitment. And, of course, these qualities are like music to every couple's ears.

Resistant to Change

Says: "Let's keep things the way they are."
Strengths: Stable, loyal, team player, and methodical
Under stress becomes: Slow-paced and inflexible
In conflict becomes: Stubborn and sullen

Accepting of Change

Says: "Let's try something new."
Strengths: Energetic, progressive, spontaneous, and flexible
Under stress becomes: Intense and restless
In conflict becomes: Distracted and impulsive

How about you? Do you tend to say, "Let's keep things the way the are," or

"Let's try something new"? Do you approach change the same way as your partner? Maybe, like us, one of you is resistant and the other is accepting of change. Once again, you probably have a hunch about where you both stand on this continuum. But we want to show you with precision just where you are and then give you the specific tools for negotiating change together successfully. Before we do that though, we have one more question for you to consider. And this last question, like the ones before it, will bring you even closer to understanding your style and enjoying Love Talk.

> Some people prefer the certainty of misery to the misery of uncertainty.
> Virginia Satir

CHAPTER EIGHT:
HOW DO YOU
MAKE DECISIONS?
CAUTIOUSLY OR SPONTANEOUSLY

We can try to avoid making choices by doing nothing, but even that is a decision.

Gary Collins

A married couple was celebrating their sixtieth wedding anniversary. At the party everybody wanted to know how they managed to stay married so long in this day and age when so many marriages don't make it. The husband responded: "When we were first married, we came to an agreement. I would make all the major decisions and my wife would make all the minor decisions. And in sixty years of marriage we have never needed to make a major decision."

That's one way to approach your decision making. It's sure to get a laugh, but it's not likely to get your relationship moving in the right direction. For in reality, it's not that simple. It takes two people to decide where they are going as a couple, which is why what seems to be simple can actually be very complex. Most couples find decision making to be one of the most excruciating aspects of their conversations. Like the previous three areas of problem solving, influencing each other, and reacting to change, decision making consumes untold hours of discussion for every couple. And determining whether you and your partner approach your decisions cautiously or spontaneously can open up a wealth of understanding for each of you, making your minor and major decisions much easier to talk about.

Allow us to begin exploring this area with you by once again revealing what we have personally learned about ourselves on the decision-making continuum.

We dated seven years before we got married. We were married fourteen years before we had our first baby. Think we struggle over our decisions? You could say that. But then again you'd only be partially right. Truth is, we are sometimes quite cautious in our decision making and sometimes quite spontaneous, since we have moderately divergent approaches as individuals on this continuum. Les is more unconventional and free-spirited in his decision making, while I'm more conventional and prudent.

Let me tell you about our engagement. I

was fourteen when we had our first date, and as I said, we dated seven years before tying the knot. We never broke up in all that time — not until we got engaged. I'll let Les take it from here.

"We need to talk" — four of the most intimidating words in a couple's vocabulary. And as soon as I heard Leslie utter them, I knew something big was brewing. We were three months into our engagement and six months away from our wedding. Her words, though softly spoken, fell with a thud on my heart.

She was serious and I was scared to death. I can't remember exactly how the drama unfolded — it's all a bit of a blur to me now — but I can recall standing in complete shock as she told me that we needed to have "space."

"Space?!" I yelped. "I'll give you all the space you need — just tell me we're still getting married."

"I can't do that." Leslie started to cry.

I cried too.

"What's this all about?" I pleaded. "I thought everything was good."

"It is good, but I just need to know for sure that I'm making this decision as much as you are," she said.

I could not have been more devastated.

More crushed. More heartbroken. Breaking up? Us? How could this be? If I hadn't known it before, I knew it now: love hurts. It is a tortuous route to finding lasting love. Of course, Leslie and I did get back together and the wedding went on as scheduled. But for the six weeks we were apart, I had never felt more alone.

If Quality Is Your Safety Need, You'll Make Decisions Cautiously

And I (Leslie) never felt more of a need to be sure my decision to get married, even after all our years of dating, was the right one. Not only is marriage a huge decision, but I also have a strong safety need for achieving quality standards. This causes me to agonize over some decisions much more than Les does. I tend to weigh the pros and cons of various ideas, and I rarely commit myself or declare my intentions until I have done so.

Let's take an example that is less emotional and weighty than marriage or having a baby, but still important. Consider buying a house or deciding where to live. A couple years ago when a realtor was showing us properties around Seattle, we came upon a lot near a golf course that we both fell in love with. There were nature trails nearby, a glimpse of the mountains. It was gorgeous. Les was ready to make an offer. Not me. I loved the property, but I needed to think about how living there would impact what schools my boys went to, where I would be in relationship to my friends.

> The cautious seldom err.
> Confucius

"Don't you have to think this stuff through?" I asked Les.

"I know we can make it work," he replied. "It's farther from the airport, but where else are you going to find a lot like this? It's great. I say we buy it before somebody else does."

"I just don't know. I love the lot, but it may change the quality of life for our boys. They won't get to go to Kings, or if they do it would be a huge commute each day for them. And it will change our social circle. We'd have to go to a different church."

You get the idea. I'm just more careful and cautious about decision making than Les is. He's more of a risk taker than me. He's also more unconventional, pioneering, and independent in his decision making. I'm more of a conformist, more likely to follow the rules and do the right thing the right way. If a dinner invitation says to arrive at 7:00, that's what I intend to do. Not Les. He may decide to get the car washed on the way to the party and be ten minutes late. It's not a big deal to him. While I feel compelled to follow rules and procedures and feel guilty when I don't, Les views rules as guidelines, mere suggestions to get him to his goal. He'd rather push the envelope, bend the rules, and ask for forgiveness rather than permission. He'll call someone late at night if he needs to talk to them, while I'd never dream of risking the chance that I might wake them up. Whether the decision is big or small, important or not, I'm more cautious and he's more spontaneous.

> Doing a thing well is
> often a waste of time.
> Robert Byrne

Keeping an Eye on the Quality Standard
If both people in a relationship are cautious decision makers, they will tend to have fewer turbulent talks about what to do when standing at a crossroads. In fact, they will

carefully weigh their options together and revel in their common concern for making the right decision in the right way. Still, this does not ensure that their decision will always be the best one (they might miss out on an opportunity while they are weighing their options). On the other hand, if two people in a relationship are both spontaneous decision makers, they may act quickly together, but this doesn't necessarily mean they will have fewer fights. After all, their spontaneity may lead them to make costly decisions they later regret or it may be about making a different decision than their partner's.[1]

Consider an example of spontaneous decision making from the world of aviation. Chuck Yeager, the famed test pilot, was flying an F-86 Sabre over a lake in the Sierras. During a slow roll, he suddenly felt his aileron lock. Says Yeager, "It was a hairy moment, flying about 150 feet off the ground and upside down."

A lesser pilot might have panicked with fatal results, but Yeager let off on the g's and pushed up the nose, and sure enough, the aileron unlocked. Yeager knew three or four pilots had died under similar circumstances, but to date, investigators were puzzled as to the source of the Sabre's fatal flaw. Yeager went to his superior with a report, and the inspectors went to work. They found that a bolt on the aileron cylinder was installed upside down.

Eventually, the source of defect was found in a North American plant. It was traced to an older man on the assembly line who ignored instructions on how to insert that bolt, because, by golly, he knew that bolts were supposed to be placed head up, not head down. In a sad commentary, Yeager says that nobody ever told the man how many pilots he had killed.[2]

It's a dramatic example, but it makes the point. We need the rules that enforce a quality standard. We need to cautiously consider our decisions. That's why the spontaneous decision maker needs to respect and honor a more cautious partner. And we'll have some specific suggestions for you in the next chapter, if neither of you is very cautious.

Cautious Decision Maker

Says: "I'm not sure yet."
Strengths: Conscientious, high standards, and accurate
Under stress becomes: Exacting and perfectionist

In conflict becomes: Indecisive and un-yielding

Spontaneous Decision Maker

Says: "Let's go for it."
Strengths: Bold, decisive, and independent
Under stress becomes: Controversial and insensitive
In conflict becomes: Reckless and overconfident

So we'll ask you one more time. What about you and your partner? Do you readily fit into one of these camps when it comes to making decisions? Are you somewhere in between caution and spontaneity? Well, it's time to find out — not only about your inclinations on decision making, but about the other three questions as well. We will show you how you can accurately identify where each of you lands on the four continuums we've been describing and how to improve your communication together once you understand this.

CHAPTER NINE:
YOUR UNIQUE TALK STYLE
TAKING THE LOVE TALK INDICATOR

Beyond the pairs of opposites of which
the world consists, new insights begin.
Hermann Hesse

Let's make sure you clearly see exactly how
your personal fear factor tends to influence
your answers to the four questions we've
just covered in the previous chapters — the
questions that determine your talk style.
If your main fear factor is the loss of . . .

- time — you'll tend to tackle problems
  aggressively rather than passively.
- approval — you'll tend to influence
  with feelings rather than facts.
- loyalty — you'll tend to be more resistant to change than accepting.
- quality — you'll tend to make decisions cautiously rather than spontaneously.

Of course, the key is to *accurately* answer

the questions we've been asking. You undoubtedly have an opinion on where you land for each of these, but we need more than an opinion to really help you. Plus, we guarantee you do not fit neatly into one extreme or the other on each of these questions (your primary fear factor determines how extreme you are on any one of them). You may be smack-dab in the middle, for example, between aggressive or passive on the problem-solving continuum. You may solve a problem aggressively in one situation and passively in another. You may be moderately aggressive or moderately passive. The same holds true for each of these questions.

Not only that, your talk style is impacted tremendously by how the four continuums interact. For example, I (Leslie) already told you I have a strong need for loyal consistency. This is a powerful value for me. The predictable makes me feel safe. But I also have a strong safety need to win the approval of others. In fact, this need often trumps my need for predictability. So I'm not always as resistant to change as you might think. Since I want people — especially Les — to like me and approve of me, I can be very spontaneous when it doesn't interfere with my most precious loyalties.

In other words, your talk style is a bit more complex than being able to simply give your opinion about how you would answer these four questions. If this is beginning to sound complicated to you, relax. We have an easy and simple way (not to mention quick) for you to accurately identify and understand your talk style. It's called the Love Talk Indicator.

Exercise 9: Identifying Your Talk Style

If you are using the accompanying workbook exercises and have access to the Internet, we suggest you use the online Love Talk Indicator described below. Once you do that, you will find some helpful discussion questions and further exploration in Exercise 9 of your workbooks.

Taking the Love Talk Indicator

Ready to discover *your* unique Talk Style? To take the Love Talk Indicator, use the personal passcode found on the inside of the back cover of this book. Once you have located it, go to **www.RealRelationships .com** and enter your passcode in the appropriate box. The on-screen instructions will walk you through it from there, and you'll soon be taking the assessment, unparalleled in helping couples understand their unique communication styles.

> This communicating of a man's self to his friend works two contrary effects; for it redoubleth joys, and cutteth griefs in half.
>
> Aristotle

To ensure accurate results, the Love Talk Indicator needs to be taken in one sitting, so be sure to set aside fifteen minutes without interruption as you prepare to take it. Upon completing the instrument, your Individual Love Talk Report will be immediately generated so you can instantly view the results and learn more about your individual talk style. Your personalized and easy-to-read report will also be ready for printing.

The Love Talk Indicator has the ability to produce 19,860 separate combinations of communication styles, each with its own unique differences. This means your report will be specific to you (see Appendix B). Of course, to maximize your assessment results, it is optimal for both you *and* your partner to take the Love Talk Indicator. You'll find more information about how easily this is accomplished on the same website. Once you both take the Indicator, you'll receive a powerful Couple's Report, clearly identifying your unique couple-communication style in which your two individual Love Talk Indicators are blended and revealing your combination of talk styles. It will show how the two of you communicate and how you can begin to almost immediately enjoy more Love Talk.

The two of you create a distinct style together, and we will show you in plain language how your individual leanings combine to create predictable patterns that, once understood, can help you steer clear of miscommunication and lead you to deeper levels of understanding. We'll also give you specific information, unique to you as a couple, about how you can minimize and more quickly resolve conflict, make decisions that are truly win-win for your individual styles, solve problems more quickly together, and most important, join your spirits by speaking each other's language like you never have before.

That's the power of taking the Love Talk Indicator and using the Love Talk Couple Report. We're convinced it will be an amazing eye-opener for both of you and will make your conversations better almost immediately.

So don't put it off. Taking the Love Talk Indicator may very well be the single most important thing you ever do to improve your communication.

■ ■ ■ ■

PART 3
ENJOYING LOVE
TALK

■ ■ ■ ■

Congratulations. You have now completed the Love Talk Indicator and have reviewed your Couple's Report to discover specific and personal ways to better communicate with each other.

With this new understanding, you are about to enjoy all that Love Talk has to give. So in this final section of the book, we take your new insights to a deeper level, beginning with the secret to emotional connection. If you don't learn it, knowing your talk styles will make little difference. We'll then help you apply your talk styles to gender differences, to listening with the third ear, to the paradox of every relationship, and finally to the most important conversation you'll ever have.

CHAPTER TEN:
TALKING A FINE LINE
THE SECRET TO EMOTIONAL CONNECTION

> A good head and a good heart are
> always a formidable combination.
> Nelson Mandela

Ladies and gentlemen, get out your calculators. According to a University of Washington study, marriage can now be reduced to an equation — the researchers claim they can "actually quantify the ratio of positive to negative interactions needed to maintain a marriage in good shape."[1] They found that "satisfied couples, no matter how their marriages stacked up against the ideal, were those who maintained a five-to-one ratio of positive to negative moments."

When Leslie and I first came upon this intriguing bit of research, I immediately knew what to do. In our kitchen, on the inside of our pantry door, you will find a dry-erase board and a felt-tip marker that serve as "communication central" for our home. If there is an important message to be relayed between us, that is where you'll find it. And it seemed to me to be the perfect spot for tabulating our conversations. I wanted to put these research findings to the test in our own marriage and see how we stacked up.

"What's this?" Leslie asked as she swung open the pantry door for a can of tomatoes. She was looking at the board where I had written at the top: "Good Talk/Bad Talk." I'd underlined the words and drawn a vertical line down the middle.

"It's a place to measure our positive/negative ratio," I said with a straight face.

"Give me a break," Leslie groaned. "You can't be serious — have you lost your mind?"

I thought for a moment, got up from my chair where I was reading the paper, and approached the board. I pulled the cap off the black marker.

"What are you doing?" Leslie asked.

"I'm putting this interaction down as a negative."

As you might guess, that was the end of my mini-experiment. So don't worry, we don't suggest you begin categorizing and tabulating your conversations. But we do recommend tapping into a component of Love Talk that promises to ratchet up your ratio of positive moments without you ever keeping track. We have seen it forever change the way hundreds of couples talk to one another. And we have seen the difference it has made for us.

The Anatomy of Love Talk

Earlier this week, we attended a memorial for Dr. Paul Brand who passed away at the age of eighty-nine. Acclaimed author Philip Yancey gave a touching and eloquent eulogy highlighting Dr. Brand's stature in the medical community: his distinguished lectureships around the world, prestigious awards, a hand-surgery procedure named in his honor, his appointment by Queen Elizabeth II as Commander of the Order of the British Empire. But after touching on these accolades, Philip devoted most of his remarks to Dr. Brand's ability to balance his towering intellect with unending kindness and humility.

Let your conversation be
always full of grace.
Colossians 4:6

In the twilight years of his career, medical schools around the globe invited him to address their students, future doctors, on the dehumanization of high-tech, HMO-driven medicine. Brand expressed the guiding principle of his medical career this way: "The most precious possession any human being has is his spirit — his will to live, his sense of dignity, his personality. Though technically we may be concerned with tendons, bones, and nerve endings, we must never lose sight of the person we are treating."

Others who had flown into Seattle for the memorial spoke of Dr. Brand's life and contributions. But it was a fellow hand surgeon who summed it up best when he said, "Paul was a man who practiced medicine with his heart as well as his head; that was his greatness."

The two words *heart* and *head* in the same sentence resonated with Les and me. We met Paul and his wife, Margaret, late in their lives, but even into their eighties this rare balancing act was obvious. So Les and I looked at each other with a knowing glance as this man made his statement. For it is this delicate balance of heart and head that makes up the anatomy of Love Talk.

When Nobel Peace Prize winner Nelson Mandela said, "A good head and a good heart are always a formidable combination," he could have been talking about intimate relationships. A couple who tunes into this powerful combination discovers a new depth in their conversations, a new way of connecting altogether.

Let's make this very clear: Our *analytical capacities* involve our ability to *think*. Your partner is working on a budget that doesn't balance. You offer help by breaking it down into causes and possible solutions. "Honey, did we buy something that didn't get recorded?" you might ask. "Is there a reason our electric bill is so high this month?" We gather information and rationally assess the problem so we can solve it. That's what analysis is all about. It comes from the head and is based on facts.

Our *sympathetic capacities,* on the other hand, involve our ability to *feel.* Seeing your partner wrestle with an unbalanced budget, you say, "I'm so sorry the columns aren't adding up for you. That's got to be frustrating. Is there anything I can do for you?" Sympathy stirs our feelings. If our partner is suffering, we feel her pain. If she is upset with the electric company, we feel her frustration. Sympathy comes from the heart and is based on feelings.

Analysis . . .
- Comes from the head
- Characterized by thinking

Sympathy . . .
- Comes from the heart
- Characterized by feeling

Whatever your unique talk style, these are the universal ingredients of Love Talk. Thinking. Feeling. It's that simple. Well, almost. Ever heard that something can be greater than the sum of its parts? This scientific axiom certainly applies to Love Talk. Once you combine thinking and feeling, head and heart, you have opened the door to the most neglected quality in meaningful conversation: Empathy.

Analysis + Sympathy = Empathy

Empathy is the centerpiece of Love Talk. No matter how you answer the four questions that determine your talk style, and no matter how much you try to practice what you learned from your Couple's Report after taking the Love Talk Indicator, you will never fully enjoy what Love Talk has to offer until you get a lock on empathy.

The Essence of Love Talk

Take any profession. Teaching second grad-
ers is a good example. You can improve a
teacher's effectiveness by having her walk
through her classroom on her knees. As she
sees that space from a second grader's
perspective, she will be better equipped to
teach them. Or how about serving fast food?
The major chains spend bundles of money
sending "fake customers" into their stores
to see it as customers do. Advertising firms
on Madison Avenue make their living by
putting themselves in the consumer's shoes.
Growing churches are growing because they
study the experience of a first-time visitor,
and the pastor imagines what it's like to sit
in the pew. Disney World's "cast members"

are trained specifically to empathize with families visiting their theme park.

Whether it be in medicine, business, education, or entertainment, *empathy* is a major component of success.[2] But it is even more essential to the success of intimate communication. Empathy — the ability to accurately see the world through your partner's eyes — is what enables a deep and meaningful connection. It allows you to literally enter your partner's experience. It's what poet Walt Whitman was getting at back in 1855 when he wrote his masterwork, *Leaves of Grass:* "I do not ask how the wounded one feels; I myself, *become* the wounded one."

Without empathy, conversation becomes the equivalent of talking on a cell phone through an intermittent transmission and an ear full of static. But when empathy enters the picture, clarity resounds with each sentence, each phrase, and each word, because your heart is resonating with emotions while your head is analyzing their accuracy. That's the quintessence of Love Talk.

Empathy is what enables you to accurately view your partner's talk style — to know why he or she is solving problems aggressively or passively, making decisions cautiously or spontaneously, and all the rest.

> If there is any one secret of success, it lies in the ability to get the other person's point of view and see things from that person's angle as well as from your own.
>
> Henry Ford

Most important, empathy is your primary tool for tapping into your partner's top emotional safety need. When you begin to recognize that your partner primarily fears losing loyalty or approval, for example, empathy catapults you into a whole new stratosphere of compassion and understanding for him or her. Empathy, in other words, ushers in grace.

"Mutual empathy is the great unsung human gift," says psychiatrist Jean Baker Miller. When a man and woman place themselves in each other's shoes, intermingling both head and heart, they discover a depth of understanding others only dream about. Once-petty problems literally fall by the wayside as they tap into what really matters, deep down, to both of them.

The effect of mutual empathy in marriage and dating relationships is staggering. Research has shown, for example, that 90 percent of our misunderstandings would be resolved if we did nothing more than see that issue from our partner's perspective. This is why empathy is the essence of Love Talk. Once you begin to practice this invaluable skill, on top of your insights about your combined talk styles, you will feel like two gold miners who have struck the mother lode. You won't believe your good fortune.

> It is only as we fully understand opinions and attitudes different from our own and the reasons for them that we better understand our own place in the scheme of things.
> S. I. Hayakawa

Okay, you say, we know empathy is important, so why is it so neglected? Empathy is not always easy since, as we've said, it demands both your head and heart, concurrently. Most of us use one or the other pretty well, but to do both can be tricky — which is exactly what empathy demands.

In case you are wondering, you're not exempt. If you are thinking some people just aren't made for empathy and you are one of them so you're off the hook, you're not. *Everyone has the capacity for empathy.* Unless you are a full-blown narcissist or a deviant with no conscience, you can use your head and heart to put yourself in your partner's place. It's been proven. Right from the beginning something in our very nature provides the makings for human empathy. When a content newborn baby hears another baby crying, for example, he also begins to wail. It's not just the loud noise, but the sound of a fellow human in distress that triggers the baby's crying.[3]

So allow us to underscore this important point: While both analyzing and sympathizing are important, neither one holds a candle to empathy — it borrows the best from both. Empathy tests the waters. It gingerly eases into a partner's predicament before trying to fix it. It says, "I know how I would feel if I were you, but I'm not you, so let me understand." And understanding is the marrow of a marriage or a dating relationship steeped in Love Talk. Empathy puts you in your partner's shoes and allows you to see the world as she sees it — through the lens of her personal fear factor. Powered by the twin engines of your head and your heart, empathy seeks to understand before being understood.

A Quick Exercise in Empathy

Take a moment right now to more fully immerse yourself in your partner's world. This will take just ten minutes or so and could very well change forever the way you view one another.

Here's how it works: Imagine, as clearly as you can, what it would be like to wake up tomorrow morning as your partner. Can you picture this? If you are married, for example, one of the first things you'd undoubtedly notice is that you'd be sleeping on the other side of the bed. If you are in a dating relationship, you'd notice that you are perhaps living in a different part of town. Can you take it from there? We urge you to take this seriously, so don't skip to the next section. We know this may sound goofy, but we have led hundreds of couples through this imaginary journey, and they almost always come away from it with a new appreciation for their partner. On one occasion, when we were doing this in our own relationship, I (Leslie) imagined what it would be like if I felt the pressure of having to pay the bills and balance the books in our home. Up to that point, I'd never given it a thought. It was "Les's job." Since I imagined what it was like, I've had a much deeper appreciation for something I completely took for granted.

So take just a few moments and imagine life as your partner through a typical day. And as you do this, keep in mind your partner's top fear factor. If he fears losing time, filter each step you take through his day with this safety need in mind. Then compare notes with each other by sharing your experience. Here's a step-by-step plan that will help you do just that.

Exercise 11: The Empathy Exercise

If you are using the men's and women's workbooks, you will find the following exercise there with a few added features. We urge you both to use the workbooks for this exercise because it will make it much more personal and meaningful.

First, close your eyes and see yourself, in your mind's eye, as your partner. Do your best to imagine what it would be like to be living in his or her skin. Next, consider a typical day and ask yourself the following questions (you may want to take a few notes on each one to compare your thoughts with your partner's notes later on).

On a typical day as your partner . . .

- What time did you get up in the morning and how did you sleep? What's your morning mood like and why?
- How long would it take you to get ready for the day? Would you spend more or less time in front of the mirror? What would you wear?
- When would you leave the house, if you left at all? What would your activities through the day be?
- What would you worry about in a typical day? What would be your likely stress points?
- What would bring you the greatest joy or satisfaction during a typical day?
- Would you have different financial responsibilities or pressures?
- Would you eat differently? Exercise? Would you be more or less concerned about your physical appearance?
- Would you feel more or less self-assured?
- How would having your partner's personal fear factor influence your interactions with others (including you)?
- How would you feel toward the end of the day as you're getting ready for dinner? What would be on your mind?
- And how would you feel about your

partner (that would be you!)? What would you want most from your partner? How would you communicate with your partner?

Congratulations on completing these questions. If you took this seriously, you undoubtedly have a unique and fresh perspective on your partner's life after doing this. Now take a few minutes to review your experience with your partner. If you took notes, compare them with each other and invite feedback on your take on life as your partner.

Finding Your Balance

Imagine yourself sixty-six feet above the ground on a platform. Now imagine taking a step, with only a half-inch metal wire between you and the ground. Welcome to the world of high wire. Centuries old, this spectacle has won world acclaim for various "rope dancers," many of whom made their name while crossing a high wire stretched over Niagara Falls. But by far the most celebrated high-wire walker is Phillipe Petit, whose unauthorized walk in 1974 between the twin towers of the World Trade Center in New York is legendary. In his book *To Reach the Clouds,* Petit describes his daring walk 1,350 feet above ground.

> Grant that I may not so much seek
> to be consoled, as to console; to be
> understood as to understand; to be
> loved, as to love.
> Prayer of St. Francis of Assisi

How does he, or anyone, maintain his balance while walking such a fine line? The answer is found in simple physics. For the high-wire performer, the wire is an axis around which a center of mass (the performer's body) can rotate. If the center of mass is not directly above the wire, the performer begins to turn and, if not corrected, will certainly fall.

The trick is to create more time for correcting the imbalance. And it *is* a trick. They call it a "balancing pole," and it may be as long as thirty-nine feet, weighing up to thirty-one pounds. This pole allows more time to move one's center of mass back to the desired position over the wire. The longer and heavier the pole, the easier it is to balance because the performer can counter-shift the pole back and forth.

In the same way, you and I can find balance between our head and our heart when we practice empathy. Empathy is the balancing pole of Love Talk. It regulates how much we sympathize and analyze. When we begin to problem-solve without regard to our partner's feelings, empathy brings us back to midline without causing a relational disaster. When we risk smothering our partner with emotional overload, empathy gets us to back off and center the conversation. Empathy, in other words, balances how much we talk with our heart and how much we talk with our head. And that's a balancing act every relationship can benefit from.

The trick, of course, is learning to find that balance in your relationship. And if you are like us, and most other couples, you know just where that balance seems to get out of whack. The problem, for most, is actually quite predictable. More likely than not, if you are the man, your Head Score is higher than your partner's. Not surprisingly, if you are the woman, your Heart Score is higher than his. This holds true, not for all, but for the vast majority of couples, which is why we devote the next chapter to helping you, as man and woman, walk confidently over the gender gap as you learn to carry the balancing pole of Love Talk.

CHAPTER ELEVEN:
MEN ANALYZE,
WOMEN SYMPATHIZE
NOW IT MAKES SENSE

Wherever people of different sexes gather, there are bound to be stress fractures along gender lines.
Deborah Tannen

When men and women refer to "conversation," they may not be talking about the same thing. Communication theorist Deborah Tannen reports a study in which students recorded casual conversations between women friends and men friends. It was easy to get recordings of women friends talking, partly because the request to "record a conversation with your friend" met with easy compliance from the students' female friends and family members. But asking men to record conversations with their friends had mixed results. One woman's mother agreed readily, but her father insisted that he didn't have conversations with his friends.

"Don't you ever call Fred on the phone?"

162

she asked, naming a man she knew to be his good friend.

"Not often," he said. "But if I do, it's because I have something to ask, and when I get the answer, I hang up."

Another woman's husband delivered a tape to her with great satisfaction and pride. "This is a good conversation," he announced, "because it's not just him and me shooting the breeze, like, 'Hi, how are you? I saw a good movie the other day,' and stuff. It's a problem-solving task. Each line is meaningful."

When the woman listened to the tape, she heard her husband and his friend trying to solve a computer problem. Not only did she not consider it "a good conversation," she didn't really regard it as a conversation at all. His idea of a good conversation was one with factual, task-focused content. Hers was one with emotional connection.[1]

And so it goes. For centuries, no doubt, long before the topic of gender studies was even conceived, men and women have been puzzled by each other's conversational competence. But one thing the genders do agree on is the supreme value of communication. Eighty-two percent of men and ninety-two percent of women say open and regular communication is "extremely important" in marriage and dating relationships.[2] So we keep trying.

This chapter is dedicated to helping you, as a man and a woman, take some of the mystery out of the gender gap. For even when you understand each other's talk style, this gap continues to exist (though your new knowledge does diminish it). We don't guarantee to solve the age-old gender puzzle in just a few pages, but we do intend to give you some practical insights for equipping you to straighten out the gender communication lines that so often get crossed. We'll explore just how different we are in conversation, and we will expose the "fundamental cross-gender relational error," an error that will trip you up every time. We then take turns at revealing in detail what men and women need to know about their respective partners.

So let's begin at the beginning with a straightforward fact: men and women are different.

Are We That Different?

I'm standing in front of our open fridge when the following dialogue takes place:

Me: "Where's the butter?"
Leslie: "It's in the fridge."

Me: "I'm looking in the fridge right now. There's no butter."

Leslie: "Well, it's there. I put it in just a few minutes ago!"

Me: "I don't see it."

Leslie: "It's in a yellow bottle, the kind you squeeze."

Me: "I know, but it's definitely not in here."

Leslie makes a beeline to the fridge and points to the butter on the second shelf.

"Oh," I say, "there it is. Where's the jam?"

Chances are you've had the same conversation. It may have been about socks, shoes, car keys, or wallets, but we've all been there. Part of the reason is found in the basic biological differences between men and women. Men's brains are pre-wired to see a much narrower field. Women's brains decode information over a wider peripheral range. Because of this, men move their heads from side to side and up and down as they scan for a desired object. With her wider arc of peripheral vision, a woman can see most of the contents of a fridge or cupboard without moving her head.

The point is, gender differences are not exclusively relegated to how you were raised as a child and society's traditional stereotyping. The differences, research is discovering, lie much deeper.

> I'd hate to think decision making was a male prerogative, or that sensitivity and nurturing were strictly for females.
> Alice Peterson

When you compare and contrast all the gender differences relevant to communication between the sexes and try to make sense of them, you will invariably risk oversimplification. We admit up front that we run this risk. But the risk is worth it. Albert Einstein once said, "Make everything as simple as possible, but not simpler." That's our goal in this chapter. So we'll temper our analogies — no comparisons of men and women being from different planets, or food groups, or species. We choose, instead, to just say it like it is: men analyze, women sympathize. It's as simple — and difficult — as that.

Not only are men's and women's brains different, but the way we use them differs dramatically. Neuropsychologist Ruben Gur of the University of Pennsylvania used brain scan tests to show that when a man's brain is in a resting state, less than 30 percent of its electrical activity is active. Scans of women's brains showed 90 percent activity during the same state, confirming that women are constantly receiving and analyzing information from their environment.[3]

For most women, it's blatantly obvious when another person is upset or feeling hurt, while a man generally has to physically witness tears or a temper tantrum before he even has a clue that anything is wrong. What is commonly called "women's intuition" is mostly a woman's acute ability to notice small details and changes in the appearance or behavior of others. And this propensity enhances a woman's sympathetic ability (her personal fear factor of losing approval can heighten this ability).

But while women have a near sixth sense for small details, their eyesight seems to change drastically when it comes to backing a car into a garage. Estimating the distance between the car fender and the garage wall while moving is, after all, a spatial skill located mainly in the right front hemisphere in men — a propensity enhancing a man's analytic ability.

Women have larger connections and subsequently more frequent "cross-talk" between their brain's left and right hemispheres. This accounts for women's seeming ability to have better verbal skills and relational intuition than men. Men on the other hand have greater brain hemisphere separation, which enhances abstract reasoning and visual-spatial intelligence. Poet and author Robert Bly describes women's brains as having a "superhighway" of connection while men have a "little crookedy country road."[4]

Big deal, you may be thinking. *Men analyze and women sympathize. How does that impact me and my partner?* We're glad you asked.

How Does This Apply to Us?

If you evaluate your partner's communication strategy according to your own standards, never considering significant social and biological differences between the genders, you will miss out on the deepest and most meaningful connections. Couples experience communication meltdowns because they are trying to get their partner to see and say things just like them — they want their partner to adopt their talk style. It's what we call the fundamental cross-gender relational error: assuming that misunderstandings between the sexes have only to do with cross-purposes and not psychological and biological crossed wiring. Remember, not only are you and your partner biologically different, but you are also wired with different talk styles that have been shaped by your genders.

Let's take a quick and classic example:

She: "I don't know how I'm going to help my mother with that party she's trying to do. All she's going to do is critique the food I bring to it anyway."

He (believing she wants a solution): "Why don't you tell her you just aren't able to help right now? Set some boundaries with her."

She (just wanting some understanding): "That's not the point. I just feel like she has always wanted me to be something I'm not when it comes to entertaining."

He: "Are you listing to me? Just tell her you can't help — get her off your back."

She: "Oh, you don't understand."

A man's relative compulsion is to solve his partner's problems. When a woman talks about her feelings, the man assumes she is seeking his help to find a solution. Like a fireman receiving a call for a fire, he jumps

Talk Styles and Gender

When it comes to the four questions that determine your talk style, two of them show significant gender differences: (1) How you tackle problems and (2) how you influence each other. (How you react to change and how you make decisions do not show a significant gender difference since there are almost an equal number of men and women who score high on each of them.)[5]

- How Do you Tackle Problems? 64% of men tend to tackle problems aggressively (as compared to passively), while only 36% of women are aggressive problem solvers.
- How Do You Influence Each Other? 63% of women influence their partner with feelings more than facts, while only 37% of men do so.

into action, quickly sizing up what it's going to take to put out the blaze. He doesn't receive a call about the fire and say, "How awful! You must *really* be hot. I'm guessing you are extremely anxious, and I'm just sorry it's so hot for you." Absurd, right? Of course.

Fear Factors and Gender

- More men (64%) identify the loss of time as their number one emotional safety need than do women (36%). This explains why more men tend to be "control freaks."
- More women (63%) identify the loss of approval as their number one emotional safety need than do men (37%). This explains why more women suffer from "the disease to please."[6]

But it seems almost as absurd to most men to listen to a woman pour out a problem without offering solutions. A man does not instinctively understand that when a woman talks about her feelings she is not seeking advice. He's not wired that way. But a woman who does not understand the "fundamental cross-gender relational error" assumes that her advice-giving partner is purely impatient with her, that he's not really listening, or that he is not interested in understanding her — just as a man who does not understand this error doesn't realize that his partner's heart would be full of appreciation and love for him if he would only respond with empathy and understanding.

Okay, I understand the problem, you are saying to yourself. *But what's the solution?* That depends on whether you are a woman or a man; either way, there are a few things you need to know. So allow us for a moment to speak to each of you individually.

For Women Only

If you are a woman reading this book, I (Leslie) know what you probably want: a conversation in which your man confides his fears, reveals his emotions, and shares his dreams. Am I close? Well, sister, you can keep dreaming (until you practice Love Talk). These heart-to-heart conversations are few and far between for most couples. The reason you may be having problems exploring your partner's emotional needs is that he doesn't *want* you to explore his emotional needs. I know, I know, it's hard to believe, but it's true. I'm not saying he doesn't feel things deeply, but, if he is like the majority of men, he certainly doesn't express his emotions as clearly and readily as you do. And who can blame him? He was raised that way. A recent study found that parents discuss emotions (with the exception of anger) more with their daughters than with their sons.[7] As adults, men naturally tend to have a smaller feeling vocabulary and stuff their emotions. The point is that we can't expect a man to identify his own emotions — let alone our emotions — as quickly as we do.

> It would be a thousand pities if women wrote like men, or lived like men, or looked like men, for if two sexes are quite inadequate, considering the vastness and variety of the world, how should we manage with one only?
> Virginia Woolf

While you and I are more likely to talk about our fears, feelings, and experiences, men are more likely to talk about ideas, concepts, and theories. Men want to tell you what they know. They use conversation to discover factual information the same way an anthropologist uses a pick and hammer to unearth an artifact. Men gather facts, debate opinions, and solve problems through reasoned conversation. Sociologist

Deborah Tannen calls this abstract style of man-speak "report talk."[8] It's well established, so in all honesty you can't expect your partner to be too enthusiastic about conversation that serves as a means with no end. You can certainly talk about fears, feelings, and dreams with him, but you can't expect him to listen all the time with the same vigilance you've grown to expect from your girlfriends.

Exercise 12: Speaking His Language

In the women's workbook you will find this exercise to be tailored to you as a woman (the exercise in the man's workbook is tailored to him). So take a moment right now to turn to this exercise and we will show you how to take this information about man-speak to a deeper level and relate it directly to your context.

For Men Only
How 'bout them Cubs?

Just kidding. Now that Leslie has had a say, allow me to turn the tables. "Every woman is a science," said John Donne. And if you take a moment to study your partner, you will discover a basic difference between the two of you that, if kept in mind, can save you endless hours of miscommunication.

Here it is: relative to you, your woman is focused on the here and now. Someone defined the future as a place where men spend most of their time. You and I both know that's not exactly true, but it becomes more true in comparison to women. While we are analyzing plans and solving problems for a better tomorrow, our partners are asking, "What's going on right now and how do the two of us feel about it?"

Women focus on current feelings and experiences because these build emotional bonds of connection between them. So while you and I are more interested in the "report" of what has happened and where we are going, our women are more interested in building "rapport" right now.[9]

As a man, I have a good idea what you want. Sex! And I'm only partially kidding this time. Truth is that, as you build a better talk life, your sex life will improve exponentially. But back to your talk life (sorry); I'm guessing your ideal conversation with your wife involves a straightforward exchange of information. If you just got home from work, for example, you want to know what the evening entails. You want to size up your options, stay on task, establish a plan, solve any problems that may interfere with its execution, and get on with it, right? No dilly-dallying. No mind reading. And certainly no processing of emotions. But hear this: if you want to get down to the task of planning your evening (or your financial future or vacation or anything else) with your wife, you must first take a moment to explore her feelings about the present. In short, before you ask what's for dinner, ask how she's doing. It doesn't have to be deep and drawn out; she just needs to know the two of you are connected and working together before you set off to achieve your goals.

Exercise 12: Speaking Her Language

In the men's workbook you will find this exercise to be tailored to you as a man (the exercise in the woman's workbook is tailored to her). So take a moment right now to turn to this exercise and we will show you how to take this information about woman-speak to a deeper level and relate it directly to your context.

These reminders for the two of you are

your insurance policy for avoiding the fundamental cross-gender relational error: assuming that misunderstandings between the two of you have only to do with cross-purposes and not psychological and biological crossed wiring. Once you remember, as a woman, that your partner is hardwired to gather a report he can analyze, and once you remember, as a man, that your partner is hardwired to build rapport where she can sympathize, you are well on your way to capturing empathy, the essence of Love Talk.

> When men and women agree, it is only in their conclusions; their reasons are always different.
> George Santayana

Generally speaking, men are concerned with getting results, achieving goals, and getting efficiently to the bottom line. Men are analytical by nature. Women are concerned with harmony and sharing; the bottom line is relevant only if it improves the relationship. Women are sympathetic by nature. Truthfully, the contrast is so great that it's amazing men and women can even speak the same language. That's what makes Love Talk — when you use your head and your heart — all the more magical.

A Quick Clarification

Before leaving you in this chapter, we have a suspicion that some of you — 10 percent to be exact — are saying, "This makes sense, but it's backwards: in our relationship he sympathizes and I analyze." And you are probably right. Research reveals that in one out of ten relationships, it is the woman who speaks more from her head than the heart and the man who speaks more from his heart than his head. This will be heightened, particularly if the woman's top emotional fear factor is losing time (and thus she is an aggressive problem solver while the man is a passive problem solver).

What's more, these people seem to find each other. Rarely is there a couple who both major in Head Talk or both major in Heart Talk. They seem to always split the difference, balancing each other out. It's God's way of helping men and women become whole, more complete. "We are each of us angels with only one wing," said Luciano de Crescenzo. "And we can only fly embracing each other."

Chapter Twelve:
Listening with
the Third Ear

CAN YOU HEAR ME NOW?

> The first duty of love is to listen.
> Paul Tillich

Erik Weihenmayer may be the world's greatest listener. On May 25, 2001, he reached the peak of Mount Everest, surely a rare and remarkable feat for anyone. But Erik is completely blind. Suffering from a degenerative eye disease, Erik lost his sight when he was thirteen. But that didn't stop him. On a mountain where 90 percent of climbers never make it to the top — and 165 have died trying since 1953 — Erik succeeded by listening. Listening very well.

Erik listened to the bell tied to the back of the climber in front of him so he would know what direction to go. He listened to the voice of teammates who would shout back to him, "Death fall two feet to your right!" so he would know what direction not to go. He listened to the sound of his pick jabbing the ice so he would know whether the ice was safe to cross. To say that Erik Weihenmayer listened as if his life depended on it is no exaggeration.

Few of us will need to depend on our listening abilities as much as Erik, but we can all learn a great lesson from his feat. Since most people talk at the rate of 120 words per minute, and since most spoken material can be comprehended equally well at rates up to 250 words per minute, there is plenty of time to be distracted from our partner's message.[1] And that's why listening is one of the single most important aspects of communication. The survivability of our conversations depends on it, and yet we take it for granted time and again. Studies have shown that most of us think we listen far better than we actually do. It's what caused Albert Guinon to say, "There are people who, instead of listening to what is being said to them, are already listening to what they are going to say themselves."

Does your partner listen attentively to what you have to say? This question, when posed to hundreds of couples, reveals that 47 percent say their partner listens attentively "some of the time," "rarely," or "never." Fifty-five percent admitted their partner accused them of not listening most of the time. More complained that their partner was easily distracted and uninterested during a conversation.[2] Yikes! Apparently we can all benefit from a little brushup on listening.

To listen is to validate, care, acknowledge, appreciate. Listening appears in so many guises that it is seldom grasped as the centerpiece of a relationship that it actually is. That's why we are compelled to include a chapter on the lost art of listening in this book. Once you uncover your personal fear factors, understand your two talk styles, and begin to empathize with one another, you are in a prime place to brush up on your listening. In fact, Love Talk will keep you at arm's length until you do just that.

So listen up. This chapter could be a major turning point in the conversations you have with each other. What we are about to share sure made a difference for us.

Listening Is Not Hearing

Okay, let's review a little Communication 101. If you can hear, you can listen — right? Wrong. Hearing is passive. Listening is active.

A sage once said that the Lord gave us two ears and one mouth, and that ratio ought to tell us something. Good point. And to drive that point home further, American psychologist Theodore Reik, one of Sigmund Freud's earliest and most brilliant students, wrote a book in 1948 called *Listening with the Third Ear.* It was his way of underscoring the fact that listening is not about hearing words. It's about hearing the message behind them.

> The most important thing
> in communication is to hear
> what isn't being said.
>   Peter F. Drucker

Consider this typical interaction between a couple stuck in traffic:

She says: If I'm late to this meeting with the board of directors, Susan is going to freak out. I have the entire proposal for this meeting with me, and she can't do a thing until I get there.

He says: Honey, I'm sure she won't be upset. People understand the traffic in this town.

This man heard his woman, but he didn't listen to her. He was more concerned with solving her problem than understanding her feelings. So she responds:

She says: You don't know Susan. I promised her I'd be there before the meeting started so we could review. I made a big deal about not being late, and this meeting is crucial. You don't understand.

He says: Hey, I'm just trying to help.

Really? Was he really trying to help? If so, he would have listened not only to his wife's words but to the anxiety behind them. He would have focused on "soothing her" rather than "solving her." He could have used a little empathy, tapped into her personal fear factor, and still tried to solve her problem, and it would have been an entirely different exchange.

He says: I know you must be anxious because of this, and I'm going to drop you off right at the door as soon as I can. Do you want to use my cell phone to call Susan?

She says: That's a good idea. Thanks for understanding, honey.

That's it. Notice that this scenario didn't take more time. It didn't require any extraneous emoting. It simply took an intentional effort to consciously feel her feelings and think her thoughts before offering a way to help her. In other words, it required his heart and head to see how her fear of losing approval (her top safety need) was impacting the conversation.

> Attend with the ear of your heart.
> Saint Benedict

You may be wondering why we keep harping on the value of empathy and noting the head/heart components. It's because most couples believe they empathize better than they do — and then they wonder why their communication isn't any better. It's not just our opinion; it's a fact. Research reveals that when couples are asked *if* they empathize with each other, they invariably say yes.[3] Okay, fair enough. But when these same couples are asked to "empathize" with characters in a story (while watching a movie, for example), a measure of their emotions reveals they aren't nearly as good at empathy as they thought they were. In fact, their understanding of the emotions the characters they were empathizing with is at the same level as those who were instructed *not* to empathize with a character's emotions. Nearly unbelievable, isn't it? But here's the part of the study that was even more surprising (and encouraging): with a little more explanation of how to empathize with the characters, the results were significantly improved. Adults who were instructed to "imagine yourself as being the other person — role-play," were far more understanding and articulate of what a character was experiencing. In other words, with just a tiny bit more help, their capacity to empathize improved dramatically.[4] That's good news for all of us.

We often tell our students at the university where we teach that sympathy is like throwing a life ring into the water to help a struggling person. Empathy, however, is like diving into that water yourself to bring them back to the shore. It's an action that will never fail to ease your partner's spirit and always draw you closer together. That's the magic of a relationship when you learn to listen with your third ear.

Listening to the Message beneath the Words

One of our favorite places on earth is the Oregon coast. It doesn't matter to us if it's dark and cloudy or bright and sunny. We'll dress accordingly and walk for miles, even in the rain, along these vast sandy shores. Most days, we find more sand dollars than

Exercise 13: Do You Hear What Your Partner Hears?

During the last ten years of Red Auerbach's coaching career, his Boston Celtics won nine National Basketball Association championships, including a record eight straight titles from 1959 to 1966. He retired at age forty-eight as the winningest coach in NBA history, with 938 victories in twenty years. A coaching genius who was known for spotting talent and getting the most out of his teams, Auerbach also knew a thing or two about communication. "It's not what you tell your players that counts," he once said, "it's what they hear." This workbook exercise will show you exactly how listening is not hearing and will prime you to get even more from the next section of this chapter.

people as we walk. But every once in a while we bump into someone with a metal detector. Wearing headphones connected to their handheld contraption, they seem oblivious to everything around them, except the message indicating whether they have discovered some buried coins or other treasures. They quietly scan the surface of the beach until it beeps in their ears. That's when they dig. Underneath the ground that most would never notice, they are drilling for riches.

You and I do the same thing when we listen to the message beneath the words of our partner. We tune in to the frequency of our third ear and quietly hear what others almost always miss. It's what linguists call the metamessage: the interpretation of intent underlying our words.

A scene from *Divorce American Style,* in which Debbie Reynolds and Dick Van Dyke are preparing dinner for guests, provides a terrific example.[5] She ignites a fight by complaining that all he does is criticize her. He's not about to take that blanket statement, and words start to fly. She says she can't discuss it right then with guests about to arrive and turns around to take bread out of the oven. That's when he asks a seemingly innocent question: "French bread?"

Seems like a simple question, an observation, really. But on hearing it, Debbie Reynolds turns on him: "What's wrong with French bread?"

"Nothing," he says. "It's just that I really like those little dinner rolls you usually make." The battle begins again. More words fly.

Did he criticize or didn't he? If you're examining only the words, no. He simply asked about the type of bread he saw her preparing. But if you consider the metamessage, he was most certainly criticizing. After all, he wouldn't even comment if her choice of bread met his standards. And because they had just been arguing about him *always* criticizing, she couldn't help but to tune in to the metamessage.

Many times, however, we're not listening to the metamessage. We're not hearing the message beneath the words. Consider this typical conversation between husband and wife:

What He/She Says

She: "How was your day?"
He: "Fine."
She: "How did your lunch with Bob go?"
He: "It was alright."
She: "Did he like your ideas about the project?"
He: "Yes."
She: "Is something wrong?"
He: "Nothing is wrong. I just need some space to unwind."

"Let's talk, I want to connect with you."

"I am giving you a short answer because I'm exhausted and need some time alone."

"I'll keep asking you questions so you know I really care about what happened to you today."

"I am trying to be polite but I want you to stop bothering me right now."

"It's okay if you don't open up right away. We can ease into this conversation and I know you will warm up soon."

"Look, you are starting to drive me nuts. I don't want to talk right now."

"You can talk to me even if you're upset. Talking will help you feel better."

"Nothing is wrong. I just need some space to unwind."

She feels hurt, says nothing, and walks away.

The skilled listener tunes in to metamessages. Consider how the above exchange could have been different if the wife would have done just that:

She says: "How was your day?"
He says: "Fine."

She says: "How did your lunch with Bob go?"

He says: "It was alright."

She says: "Would you like some time to regroup before we connect on your day?"

He says: "Honey, that would be great. Thanks."

Or how about if the husband would have tuned in to the metamessages of his wife. It may have gone like this:

She says: "How was your day?"

He says: "Fine."

She says: "How did your lunch with Bob go?"

He says: "It was alright. I want to tell you all about it, but would you mind if I decompress by watching the news before we do that?"

She says: "Sure. We can talk over dinner."

Listening with the third ear works wonders. When you do this, when you listen thoughtfully to the message beneath the words, you'll be amazed by what it does for your relationship.

Exercise 14: Reading Your Partner's Body Language

A big part of tuning in to the metamessage in any conversation is getting a read on the other person's body language. It can speak volumes. Shakespeare understood this when he said, "There's language in her eye, her cheek, her lip, Nay, her foot speaks; her wanton spirits look out at every joint and motive of her body." In this workbook exercise we reveal the telltale signs you may be missing in your partner's communication. We show you exactly what to look for and what it means when you see it.

What Listening Does for a Relationship

Ben Feldman, the first insurance salesman to pass the sales goal of $25 million in one year, had a simple formula for his success. He was New York Life's leading salesman for more than twenty years, operating out of East Liverpool, Ohio, a city of 20,000. His secret was to work hard, think big, and listen very well. Many in Ben's profession identify with the first two qualities of his success. But it's that third one — listening well to his potential customers — that trips up the majority. Only those in the top percentiles of sales really put listening skills into practice.

> Be quick to listen and slow to speak.
> James 1:19

Countless articles have put the spotlight on the benefits of listening in the business world. One study revealed that hourly employees spend 30 percent of their time listening, while managers spend 60 percent, and executives 75 percent or more.[6] Does effective listening lead to promotion, or do higher-ups learn to listen better because they must? It is probably a combination. Essentially, to be more successful, you must be a better listener.

And the same holds true in marriage. Your relational success increases in direct relation to the effectiveness with which you listen to each other. "The road to the heart," wrote Voltaire, "is the ear." And listening with the third ear puts you squarely on the path to deeper intimacy. It bridges any space between you.

Tina, married for eight years, was shriveling up in her marriage. Rick, her husband, tuned her out. She told us he turned on the TV during dinner, blared talk radio in their car, called clients on his cell phone, anything and everything but connect with Tina.

When they came to our counseling office, Rick, a Texas transplant to Seattle, was resistant, to say the least. They sat in swivel chairs across the coffee table from Les and me. Rick mostly shifted his gaze between the two of us when he talked, but he looked straight at me, as if he were trying to get a read on my female sympathies for his wife, when he said, "I don't go in for this counseling business, but Tina twisted my arm."

Les assured him it would be relatively painless. And then, to back up his words, we threw out a challenge: "We're going to give you one simple assignment between now and next week, and if it doesn't make a significant difference in your relationship, we'll call it quits."

"That's a risky offer to a man who's looking for an excuse not to be here," Rick said with a drawl. "But I'm game."

The assignment was straightforward. Spend ten minutes a day, for the next seven days, in a conversation in which you do nothing but focus on each other. No phone calls, no TV, just talk about anything you want.

"That's the problem: We don't have anything to talk about," Rick protested.

"Then just listen while Tina talks."

Rick agreed that he could do that. We role-played a few scenarios until we were confident they both understood, then we sent them on their way.

Next time we saw Rick and Tina there was a visible difference. Tina's countenance had changed. Rick was all smiles.

"Doc," he said, "listening made all the difference."

Tina started to tear up.

"We did just like you said. I listened. That's it. But by the third day I realized how alone Tina felt in our marriage, and it changed me. She deserves better." Rick cleared his throat, not about to get choked up, and said, "And she's going to get better. I'm going to listen to her like I'm listening for a lost watch in the icehouse."

We couldn't help but chuckle at his colorful phrase. But clearly, he got the point. That was years ago. And we've never forgotten the way Rick said it.

There is curative power in listening. Years of hurt and harm from feeling isolated can be washed clean when a man or a woman genuinely listens with the third ear. Catherine de Hueck put it nicely when she said,

"With the gift of listening comes the gift of healing." And it does.

The Worst Listening Mistake You'll Ever Make

"Have you seen this catalog?" Les asked while I was mixing baby formula at the kitchen counter.

"What catalog?"

"This Brooks Brothers catalog — why don't you order some things? Order anything you want; looks like it's all on sale."

On nearly any other day, I would have been dialing that 800 number and rattling off catalog codes to the operator as fast as I could. But this was not my most shining moment. I was just recovering from a difficult pregnancy and couldn't help but hear Les's invitation to order clothes this way: "It's high time you whip yourself into shape, drop the mommy wardrobe, and get some clothes that make you look better." Granted, he didn't utter a word of this; in fact, he didn't even think a thought of it. Les simply wanted me to enjoy a little shopping spree in one of my favorite catalogs while they were having a winter sale. I know this because we spent the next hour and a half talking about how I misread his message.

> He had occasional flashes of silence, that made his conversation perfectly delightful.
> Sydney Smith

"What's wrong?"

"I feel so bad about myself, and now you think I don't look pretty anymore," I said as tears began to trickle down my face.

"What are you talking about?" Les asked.

His shock was genuine, but it didn't stop my tears. My lousy feelings were determined to reinvent what he had said to me.

"I just thought there were some pretty good deals in here, and if I knew how to choose the ones you like best in the sizes you want, I'd do it for you — as a gift," Les said.

"So you're afraid I can't wear the same things I used to," I said with an accusatory tone.

"Hey, you're putting words in my mouth. I didn't —"

"Can't you see I feel terrible about the way I look?" I interrupted. "I don't need to buy clothes I can't even wear. Do you see any postpartum models in that catalog?"

"I promise I wasn't sending you a message," Les said with a gentle voice. "I genuinely thought you would enjoy some new things, that's all."

As we unpacked my emotional misreading, I eventually heard Les's true message. But it took awhile because my invented words were more powerful than the ones he had spoken.

> You cannot truly listen to anyone
> and do anything else at the same
> time.
>
> M. Scott Peck

Ever had a similar experience? Dumb question, we know. Every couple does this on occasion. Take our friend, Chuck Snyder, who was placing a chunk of cheese on a cracker and zapping it in the microwave when his wife, Barb, walked by.

"That's too big," she said.

What Chuck heard was "Hey, fatso, are you really going to eat that huge piece of cheese by yourself?"

In truth, all Barb was saying was that the cheese was too big to melt properly. It would need to be cut into smaller chunks.

Reading an imagined meaning into a partner's message is perhaps the most lethal mistake we make when it comes to listening. It turns our conversation, in effect, into an inkblot test in which we project our own fears and frustrations onto an otherwise harmless dialogue.

But there's a solution.

Let Me Read Your Mind

If you're tired of misreading your partner's intentions, if your listening skills in this area are lagging, try something we started nearly a decade ago. It's an exercise called "Let Me Read Your Mind." Don't worry; it doesn't require you to sit on the floor swami style and wear a funny hat.

When either one of you is running the risk of reading something into a message that isn't there, say, "I'd like to read your mind." When your partner agrees, you tell him or her what it is you are hearing. Don't pass judgment at this point; just reveal what you perceive. You are not giving validity to the message at this point; you're just seeing if it's correct. Next, your partner simply rates how accurate (or inaccurate) you are on a scale of one to ten — ten being right on the money. Here's an example:

She says: "I'd like to read your mind."
He says: "Be my guest."
She says: "Last night at dinner when you

made that joke about the number of minutes I used on my cell phone, you were thinking that I spend too much time talking to my sister. Am I right?"

He says: "That's about a three. The thought went through my head, but not for long. I was really wondering if we should get a new phone plan if you use that many minutes every month."

Or consider an example of a couple who is thinking about a major move across the country because of a new job offer:

He says: "I'd like to read your mind."
She says: "Okay."
He says: "I think that even though you say you are willing to move our family to Philadelphia, you really want to stay put. I think you're afraid of disappointing me or holding my career back. Am I right?"
She says: "Yes. That's about an eight or nine. You're right. I'm afraid to speak up on this because I know you are excited about this opportunity."

You get the idea. This exercise cuts through all the smoke and mirrors of a relationship shrouded by misinterpreted messages. It allows you to put your fears and frustrations on the table to see if they're valid. Think of the time and energy you can save with this technique! But remember, it will fall flat if you're not operating from a base of empathy, genuinely wanting to understand your partner.

Exercise 15: I Want to Read Your Mind

You may be thinking that you will try this little exercise of "mind reading" sometime. Great! But don't wait. If you really want to put it into practice, try it right now. The workbook exercise will walk you through a current issue in your relationship. Go ahead and try it. You'll soon see how well it works and how easy it is to do.

Did You Hear What I Said?

In his book *Stress Fractures,* Chuck Swindoll tells of a day when he learned an important lesson about listening. He was caught in the under-tow of too many commitments in too few days. He found himself snapping at his wife and children. He was rushing though mealtimes and feeling irritated by any unexpected interruption to his schedule. His hurry-up demeanor was becoming unbearable.

"I distinctly recall after supper one evening, the words of our younger daughter, Colleen," he writes. "She wanted to tell me about something important that had happened to her at school that day. She hurriedly began, 'Daddy-I-wanna-tell-you-somethin'-and-I'll-tell-you-really-fast.' "

Chuck, suddenly realizing her frustration, answered, "Honey, you can tell me . . . and you don't have to tell me really fast. Say it slowly." Then he says, "I'll never forget her answer: 'Then listen slowly.' "

Out of the mouths of babes, right? Listen slowly. It's good advice for all of us. We seldom realize the tremendous gift we can offer each other when we take a moment to listen not only to each other's words but to each other's feelings behind the words. Listening with the third ear is, pure and simple, the gift of understanding.

Renowned Swiss counselor Dr. Paul Tournier has said, "It is impossible to overemphasize the immense need we have to be really listened to, to be taken seriously, to be understood. . . . No one can develop freely in this world and find a full life without feeling understood by at least one person."[7] When you offer your partner the gift of listening, you are embodying what your relationship was meant to be.

CHAPTER THIRTEEN:
WHEN NOT TO TALK
THE PARADOX OF EVERY RELATIONSHIP

> Well-timed silence hath more
> eloquence than speech.
>   Martin Fraquhar Tupper

Stop talking. We mean it.

This may sound strange coming from two relationship specialists, but we're serious. Stop talking. This may sound like unorthodox advice, but not only is silence golden, it's also vital to good communication.

Having a tug-of-war with your partner about where to go on your next date? Whether to relocate for a new job opportunity? Or how to discipline your kids? Ask anyone with an opinion and they will tell you the same thing: "You've got to talk it through." Okay, we'll buy that — but only at a good price. We won't buy it if the cost outweighs the benefit, which is why we say there are times when a couple simply needs to clam up.

We agree that the way to solve problems

in your relationship is to talk about them. But there can also be power and wisdom in not talking — in biding your time, walking away, or just simply shutting up and getting on with things.

Now, I (Les) can almost hear some of you men reading this and saying to your partner, "See there, honey, we don't need to discuss everything." You're thinking we just gave you a new pony to ride out of the conversational corral. Well, slow down, partner. It's not like that, but I think you're still going to appreciate what we have to say here.

And I (Leslie) can hear some of you women reading this initial advice and saying to yourself, "What kind of a book is this — I thought it was suppose to open up the communication channels, not shut them down." I understand, but stay with us on this. You'll discover that what we are suggesting will actually make your communication more rich and intimate.

You see, there are select times and places in every relationship to stop talking, if only briefly, and this chapter is dedicated to helping you pinpoint each one of them. While we obviously believe in talking it through, there are at least seven specific times when you need to be silent. Chances are, you already know a few of them. In fact, right here at the outset, we have an exercise in the workbooks to heighten your awareness of this issue.

Exercise 16: Is It Time to Clam Up?

Before moving forward, take a quick quiz to see how well you intuitively know when a conversation needs a timeout. This workbook exercise will present you with some common scenarios to assess. No sneaking a peak a the rest of this chapter first, if you want this exercise to give you a good and honest take on your ability here.

---

1. Stop Talking When One of You Isn't Ready

Wife: "We need to figure out how we're going to handle child care for Thursday night when we go to Jeff's banquet."

Husband (while balancing a checkbook): "What?"

Wife: "Sarah can't watch the kids but Amy can. But the boys are never well behaved when Amy watches them. Don't you think we should pass on Amy?"

Husband (eyes still on the checkbook):

"Umm, what's this about now? Amy who?"

Wife: "Sarah can't watch the kids."

Husband (making eye contact): "When?"

Wife: "Why don't you ever listen to me?"

He may not be listening because you're talking when he isn't ready. I (Leslie) have learned and relearned the price of this mistake. I can't count the times I have tried to converse with Les when he was in the middle of a task and I ended up getting my feelings hurt. So take it from me, if you have something on your mind and your partner isn't ready to talk about it, clam up. Let him or her know you want to talk. Say something like, "I need to talk to you about child care when you're ready; will you have some time before dinner?" That's all it takes to make sure your partner's mind is in a receptive space.

2. Stop Talking When You've Said It a Million Times

If you've been telling him for eight years not to put his jacket on the back of the dining room chair and he's still doing do it, or you've been arguing for four summers about whether or not to buy an expensive barbe-

cue grill, it might be time to take a perma-
nent break from the conversation. At some
point you need to realize that talking is not
going to provide the solution.

> Silence is one of the
> great arts of conversation.
>   Tom Blair

If you've locked horns on replacing your
washer and dryer or on how much money
to give to a charitable cause, you might
simply have to agree to disagree. You may
be able to work out a compromise that will
at least partly satisfy you both. Or maybe
you go on as you have been and agree to
table all discussion on the matter for, say,
the next six months.

The point is that if your conversations are
getting you nowhere, you need to give it a
rest. Of course, in some cases, there are ac-
tions you can take that *do* speak louder than
words. If you've asked, cajoled, threatened,
and analyzed your man on the subject of
not hanging up his coat in the closet, and
he keeps promising to do so but never does,
you have some options: (a) you could decide
to hang it up for him and say no more about
it; (b) you could leave it there and say noth-

ing; or (c) you could hide his jacket each time he leaves it in an undesirable spot. This last option is for those with a mean streak (we don't recommend it), but we want to give you all the options here. The only option not available to you is to keep talking about it.

The bottom line is that you need to give up the conversations you keep having over and over and over. They will grind both of you down.

3. Stop Talking When You Need Time to Think

"Power stalling." It's not a phrase you'll read about in other romantic relationship books, but it's a technique we've learned to love in our own relationship. And we learned it from the world of business. We were talking with a friend over dinner who works as a management consultant. He told us that "power stalling" is common practice in every company, and he asked if we used it in our marriage work. We were intrigued.

"On the job," he said, "if someone runs a new idea past you in the hall, you say, 'That's interesting. Let me think about it.' But somehow if my wife runs one past me, I'm apt to yell, 'You know, I don't like that.' It's like I become five years old at home."

We immediately knew what he meant. And you probably do too. The idea of reining in our feelings is anathema to most married couples. If he proposes a white-water-rafting trip, you come back immediately with a tirade of how you've had your heart set on a resort. You hate camping. If she proposes an outing to a friend's cantata, you hurl back protests of how boring it would be and how you don't even know her friend. You hate cantatas.

But wait. Why approach it like a five-year-old? Instead, why not say, "Let me think about it and get back to you"? This buys you a cooling-off period, time to weigh how you really feel about something without the pressure of having to give a spontaneous reply and time to compose a thoughtful response.

This works just as well when you're the one with something to talk about. In fact, we often coach each other on this strategy by saying something like, "I want to talk to you about an idea, but I don't want you to respond immediately." This is a way of getting an idea or suggestion on the table without getting clobbered for bringing it up.

4. Stop Talking When One of You Is Being Unreasonable

Maybe her boss yelled at her. Maybe she had a bad interaction with her mother. Whatever the explanation, you've initiated a discussion about finances, and she starts shrieking about your attitude and how you're attacking her. "You're always criticizing me, and you never appreciate what I do for you."

> There is not only an art, but an eloquence in silence.
> Cicero

At this point, the wisest tack is not to discuss either the new budget or her bizarre behavior, but to say as calmly as you can, "I'm going to give you some space right now." You don't need to be judgmental. Just set a boundary by clamming up until a little sanity enters the picture.

Of course, the same holds true when the shoe is on the other foot. When you're feeling a little insane and your emotions are like a ticking time bomb, you need to give yourself some space.

Too many couples try to have rational conversations when one of them is in an irrational space. It never works. So the next time one of you is being unreasonable, hold off on conversing and provide a space for sanity. As Benedictine monk Peter Minard put it: "Silence begins when a reasonable being withdraws from the noise in order to find peace and order in his inner sanctuary." Once you have both taken a bit of refuge in quietness from each other, you're bound to have a more reasonable conversation.

5. Stop Talking When You've Forgotten the Problem You Were Talking About

Les and I were having a reasonable conversation about how to arrange the furniture in what was intended to be our formal living room. With the addition of a second baby and soon-to-be toddler to our family, we both agreed it was time to convert the room into a play space. But as we jockeyed the furniture around, we realized some pieces would have to go.

"I've never really liked that antique table we put all the pictures on," said Les.

"You're kidding?!" I quickly responded. "That's my favorite piece of furniture in the house."

"You like it because you like the pictures on it," Les protested.

"Excuse me — I know what I like, and I like the table."

"Well, we could keep the table and put the toys on top of it," Les quickly suggested.

"Why don't we get rid of your bookshelf?" I countered.

"Suddenly it's *my* bookshelf, huh?"

"Well, you know I never wanted it in here," I said.

"Well, what about the painting upstairs I can't stand?" asked Les.

"The one your parents gave us? That's your issue."

"Okay, you want to bring parents into this discussion. . . ."

"Wait a second, time out, what are we doing? What are we even talking about?" I asked.

Ever had one of those? What couple hasn't? We've all had conversations that get derailed. You start out talking about what color to paint the kitchen, and suddenly you're fighting about ice cream and the proper temperature for setting the freezer knob.

When you can no longer remember what exactly you're trying to decide, when you have to ask "What are we arguing about?" take a timeout and cool down. We have a phrase for helping us do just that in our own

211

relationship: "Let's cool our heads and warm our hearts." This simple reminder keeps us from being swallowed by a conversation that has turned silly and is bordering on becoming vicious.

6. Stop Talking When You're Spewing Advice

Last week we had a speaking engagement in Oklahoma City. The couple who picked us up at the airport were exceptionally kind — to us and each other. Maybe too kind. On the way to the venue, with time being critical, the husband unknowingly took a wrong turn. We drove for a few minutes in that direction when he said, "I think I was supposed to go left back there." That's when his wife said, "Yes, I knew you were to go left on 109th, but I didn't want to say anything."

What?! Didn't want to say anything? Les nearly came unglued. He restrained himself and politely asked why.

"I didn't want to embarrass my husband, and I knew he'd eventually figure it out," she told him.

Her answer did little to sooth Les, but it did highlight an interesting relational strategy, even if taken to the extreme. You see, most of us are quick on the trigger when it comes to advice for our spouse.

> I have often regretted my speech,
> never my silence.
>
> Publilius Syrus

"You need to pick up your socks."

"You left the hall light on again."

"You're going to be late if you don't pick up the pace."

Comments like this rarely do any good. They're said in a vain attempt to change our partner, but they are about as helpful as a raincoat when it's not raining. Nobody likes unsolicited advice and critique, but most of us can't help showering it upon our partner. So the next time your advice-giving is in full throttle, do what you can to curb it. Shut it down. And if you can't restrain yourself, make it easier to hear by saying, "I know you didn't ask for my advice, but can I tell you what I'm thinking?"

7. Stop Talking When You're Talking to Avoid Doing

"Delay is the deadliest form of denial," said Professor Northcote Parkinson. In fact, he's famous for this curious line. At a tea in his honor he was asked to explain this saying.

Exercise 17: Enough Advice Already!
We all know the common stereotype: a woman brings a problem to the man and the man immediately tries to fix it. Okay, so it's true. At least a lot of the time. But don't think for a minute that men have a monopoly on giving unwanted advice. In fact, some research has shown that women are more prone than men to give a critique of their partner's behavior. So what can we do? Plenty. This exercise in the workbooks will give you an opportunity to curb unwanted advice — from both you and your partner.

"I will," replied Parkinson, "in a few minutes."

You get the point. Truthfully, anyone who is substituting conversation for taking action is in denial. Whenever we talk about something we need to do instead of actually doing it, we make believe we are getting closer to taking action. But we aren't. Hang around a group of commiserating graduate students who are going on and on about the travails of writing a dissertation, and you'll see how much they could have written if they'd have simply stopped talking about it and done it.

The same holds true in a marriage and the subject of sex is a good example. When partners begin talking about why they're not having much sex in their marriage, their very conversation can keep them from acting at all. It creates more pressure. Their lack of sex has now become an "issue." And issues need to be explored, right? So they look at every side of the issue and become more inactive with each paragraph of conversation. They fall victim to the "paralysis of analysis." Their discussions lead to terminal inaction. In the time they spend talking about why they're not making love, they could be making love.

Of course, it's not always that simple, but it often is. So if you're using your conversation to avoid doing something, don't delay. Don't live in denial. Stop stewing and start doing.

We've provided a capsule summary of the seven times in every relationship in which silence is not only golden, but necessary.

Stop Talking . . .

When one of you isn't ready.
When you've said it a million times.
When you need time to think.

When one of you is being unreasonable.

When you've forgotten the problem you were talking about.

When you're spewing advice.

When you're talking to avoid doing.

By Saying . . .

"I need to talk to you when you're ready; will you have some time before dinner?"

"I'm not going to talk about this subject for the next six months."

"That's interesting. Let me think about it."

"I'm going to give you some space right now."

"Let's cool our heads and warm our hearts."

"I know you didn't ask for my advice, but can I tell you what I'm thinking?"

"Enough said, let's do this."

Breaking the Silence

William Penn, the founder of Pennsylvania, was imprisoned during the seventeenth century for his Quaker beliefs. And while in prison, he wrote something that sparked a thought in us as we turn our attention to concluding this chapter. "True silence," he said, "is like rest for the mind." Indeed. And we would add that silence is to conversation what sleep is to the body. A moment of quiet reflection at the right time nourishes and refreshes the spirit of Love Talk.

But just as sleeping too much is a symptom of potential problems, too much silence in a relationship is certainly problematic. So lest we be misunderstood, we want to underscore the value of talk. The point of this chapter is to identify the specific times when and places where conversation is not necessary and is even hurtful in a relationship, but the overarching goal, of course, is to bring about more productive, meaningful, and intimate conversations between the two of you.

CHAPTER FOURTEEN: LET'S TALK LOVE

THE MOST IMPORTANT CONVERSATION YOU'LL EVER HAVE

> What you do speaks so loudly that I cannot hear what you say.
> Ralph Waldo Emerson

The world's longest marriage was celebrated recently. Lee, 91, and Kim, 95, from Korea set a global record, according to the *Guinness Book of Records,* when they celebrated their eighty-second wedding anniversary at a festive event in the house of their first son, aged 75.[1] Lee and Kim have five sons and three daughters and 105 grandchildren and great-grandchildren. On their anniversary, the world's longest married couple was given special gifts, including 82 roses — and hearing aids.

After more than eight decades of marriage, they were getting hearing aids! Guess they wanted to be sure they still wouldn't miss a word. Can you imagine the number of conversations this couple has had? In all that time, they must have touched on every conceivable topic a husband and wife could talk about. But this record-breaking marriage got us to thinking. We wonder if Lee and Kim ever paid conscious attention to a conversation they may not have even known they had. Few couples do.

Every day you are together — whether you are dating or married — there is a quiet conversation that almost always goes unnoticed. Yet the content of this conversation is the most important discussion a couple ever has. Its words linger longer, are felt more deeply, and carry more clout than either partner could ever imagine. This conversation, more than any other, determines the closeness or distance they feel.[2] Ultimately, this conversation decides whether a couple will truly enjoy Love Talk, whether they will speak each other's language like they never have before.

We're talking about the conversation you have with yourself when your partner isn't listening. We're talking about your relational self-talk.

Imagine that at the end of each week you slip a microchip into a computer and it tabulates and categorizes everything you said to yourself about your spouse. And imagine that the same computer would do the same thing for everything you said about yourself. It would spit out a record of all your internal dialogue that pertains to your relationship. And now imagine you and your partner sitting down to study it. What would you find?

First, you would almost certainly be surprised if you listened in. You might find, for example, that you are giving your partner internal compliments he or she never hears. *I love it when she wears that dress. He's brilliant with kids.* But you may also be shocked to find how much negative commentary you quietly grumble about him or her. *He cares more about his car than me. She's so careless with money.* Not only that, you might be astonished to learn how many negative things you're saying to yourself about you. *I'm so selfish. I was a real jerk. I should have known better. I'm such an idiot.* This kind of self-talk sets up impossible standards and then tears you down for not meeting them. It calls you names: stupid, incompetent, ugly, selfish, weak. Your negative inner voice tells you that you're a lousy mate, that your partner is annoyed or disgusted. Your pathological critic, if not tamed, will undermine your dignity at every turn. And according to some experts, as much as 77 percent of the average person's self-talk is negative.[3] Imagine the impact this has on a marriage

— how it ultimately hinders Love Talk.

> We act upon our thoughts. These thoughts literally become our daily life experience.
>
> Wayne Dyer

Your internal dialogue about your relationship is like a prism through which all your verbal conversations are refracted. If you neglect this covert conversation, you'll forever struggle to get the overt dialogue with your spouse right.

So we dedicate this chapter to helping you tune in to your self-talk as it relates to your relationship, and we begin by uncovering its origins.[4] We show you how your brain, deep down in its many folds and crevices, holds the most important conversation you ever have. We also define exactly what self-talk is. We'll show you how to accurately assess your internal dialogue by zeroing in on the two hinges upon which Love Talk hangs. And finally, we will leave you with a simple but meaningful exercise for improving your self-talk.

Your Brain Has a Mind of Its Own

The brain is the only organ of the body totally essential for individual identity. If you have a defective kidney or liver, or even heart, you can acquire a transplant and still retain your sense of self. But if you were to acquire a new brain, you would acquire a new personality. You would have a different set of memories, a different vocabulary, different aspirations. You would experience different emotions. With a new brain you acquire a new mind. In short, assuming that medical science could solve the incredibly complex problems involved in a brain transplant, you would be somebody else in the same skin. The power of the human brain is unmistakable. It does nothing less than preside over who you are.

And that is precisely why self-talk is paramount to becoming the person you want to be. At the risk of oversimplifying the majesty of the mind, you can think of it as being composed of intricate internal conversations. The brain is a circuitry of complex communication relaying millions of messages at any moment.[5] And these messages determine who you are. They have a direct impact, not only on your body, but on your spirit as well. Your very personality — what you do and how you come across

— is defined by your internal messages.

Stay with us on this. Your psychological state, and thus the state of your relationship, is played out through a series of electrochemical connections in your brain. In other words, you prescribe, to a large degree, what your brain does by what you say when no one's listening. And over time, the secret messages you shoot repeatedly through your mind begin to cut a groove or wear a path through your cortex.[6] The routine and habitual nature of these messages make them prominent. They achieve a higher priority than others. These governing messages, the ones that are heard most loudly, most often, and most quickly, are the ones that define your self-talk — and thus your relationship.

What Is Self-Talk?

Each of us, every minute of every hour, is holding an unending dialogue with ourselves, a dialogue that colors every experience — especially our dating or marriage relationship. The dialogue has been compared to a waterfall of thoughts cascading down the back of our minds. The thoughts are rarely noticed, but they continually shape our attitudes, emotions, and outlook.

Self-talk is typically not spoken aloud, but

its message is more piercing than any audible voice. What's more, it is reflexive. Automatic. Self-talk occurs without any prior reflection or reasoning. Our brain instantly sees it as plausible and valid. Our self-talk need not be accurate. In fact, for many of us, it rarely is. But it never hinders the mind from acting as if it were.

In 1955 a little-known professor of psychology at Rutgers University was building a counseling practice but growing increasingly disillusioned with the traditional methods of treatment. Psychoanalysis, in his opinion, was too costly, too long, and too out of touch with how people change. So he gave up psychoanalysis entirely and began his own brand of therapy with the founding of his Institute for Rational Living. Albert Ellis, the now ninety-year-old founder, still travels the country holding workshops on his famed Rational-Emotive Therapy. Ellis was the first to use the term *self-talk*. Today, of course, it is part of common vocabulary and there are several qualities that define it.

Self-Talk Is Personal and Specific

Judy has been married four years. Last night at dinner she asked her husband, Bill, if he'd like to take a walk around the neighborhood after their meal. Bill said he'd rather read the paper. This stopped Judy right in her tracks. *He doesn't really enjoy my company,* she said to herself. Notice that Judy did not say, *He's probably tired after working so hard,* or even *His knee may be bothering him.* She zeroed in on one specific thought that relates to her: *Bill doesn't want to be with me.*

Self-Talk Is Concise

It is often composed of just a few words or even a brief visual image.[7] *Latte in O'Hare.* When I (Les) let these three words slip into the crevices of my cortex, they immediately engender inadequacy. They remind me of a time when I was a real jerk as a husband — when I didn't want to buy a measly cup of overpriced coffee while we were traveling. Since then, whenever I'm starting to make a selfish decision that impacts my wife (a time when I'm about to nix a small act that would let Leslie know I cherish her), these three words creep up on me and immediately pull me down. That's the nature of self-talk. It is concise. One word or a short phrase becomes shorthand for a group of self-reproaches, fears, or memories.

> Self-respect is the cornerstone of all virtue.
>
> John Herschel

Self-Talk Is Quick and Spontaneous

You're driving around town, running some errands, when you spot your husband at a Ticketmaster window. *He's buying tickets to a ball game with his buddies,* you say to yourself without hesitation. You immediately get worked up. After all, you see him with your own eyes, joking with his friends over his lunch hour. *That is so like him,* you say in disgust. *He doesn't even consider how that might impact my schedule.* You stew about it all afternoon, and as your anger builds you know just what you are going to say to him at home. The minute you see him, you snap loudly: "You could have asked me first!" Obviously surprised, your husband says, "Asked about what?" That's when you let him have it by revealing you caught him red-handed. "Oh, honey," he says, "I wanted to surprise you." *Surprise me? What?* "I knew you wanted to see *My Fair Lady* while it was in town, so during my lunch hour I got us tickets for tomorrow night." It's the nature of self-talk to waste no time in rushing to judgment.

Self-Talk Is Believed, No Matter How Irrational

We had just stepped off the platform in a lecture hall at our own university. I (Les) was packing up my briefcase and answering a few questions from students. I was ready to go when I noted that Leslie had at least a dozen students gathered around her. "Dr. Parrott," I heard one student say to her, "what you said tonight really helped me." Other students who were gathered around nodded in agreement and then asked a few follow-up questions to the lecture. Once we finally left the auditorium, I asked, "So how do you think it went?" That's when Leslie surprised me: "I really missed the mark," she said. Of course, I countered with a heavy dose of praise and reminded her of what the students had just said. But let me tell you, if she or anyone else believes her own self-talk ("I did a terrible job"), messages to the contrary can do little good. If someone feels she didn't meet her own standards, she can convince herself she failed. Irrational? You bet. But that's self-talk.

> The first order of business of anyone who wants to enjoy success in all areas of his or her life is to take charge of the internal dialogue they have.
>
> Sidney Madwed

Self-Talk Is Learned

Cindy grew up in a very proper home. Her father, for example, would always open doors for her mother. In fact, her mom would sit in the passenger's side of the car until her dad walked around to her side to open it for her. *That's how a man shows his wife he loves her,* little Cindy would think to herself. Who wouldn't? But as you might guess, when Cindy got married, her husband never considered such an "old-fashioned notion." "That's why we have power locks," he'd joke with his new wife. But a quiet voice inside Cindy's head would say, *If he really cherished me, he'd open my car door.* Of course, Cindy wouldn't be saying that if she hadn't seen it throughout her childhood. She learned it, just like we've all acquired self-talk based on our upbringing. This aspect of self-talk, however, is the most encouraging: if irrational self-talk can be learned, it can be unlearned too.[8]

To sum up, self-talk, the automatic thoughts that cut a groove in our brain, is personal and specific, concise, quick and spontaneous, believed, and learned. With this understanding, we now turn to how these silent statements, the ones that are heard most loudly, most often, and most quickly, help or hinder our Love Talk.

Exercise 18: Tuning In to Your Self Talk

The most important step toward using self-talk to your advantage is becoming aware of what you are actually saying to yourself. Once you become aware of your internal dialogue, you can do something about it. This workbook exercise is designed to help you do just that. It will present you with a series of scenarios and then ask you to choose from among several typical responses. Your responses will reveal a great deal about what you say to yourself when no one's listening.

Your Governing Relationship Message
Press the rewind button on your mental tape player. Review a conversation you had

with your partner today. It may have been this morning as you were getting ready for work. Perhaps it was over the phone or around dinnertime. Replay as much of the conversation as you can. Now rewind your mental tape player to review the messages you sent yourself during that same interchange. Are those conversations coming to mind as readily? Not if you are like most people. Most of us recall far more clearly the words we speak aloud than the words we speak to ourselves.

Still, our internal conversation *is* real. While we speak out loud at the rate of 150 to 200 words per minute, research suggests that we talk privately to ourselves at the rate of approximately 1,300 words per minute. And this internal conversation is never turned off; it even runs while we sleep, monitoring and influencing our dreams.

The point is that you may not always be aware of your internal dialogue, but that doesn't stop it from shaping your relationship. And that doesn't have to stop you from doing something about it. The key, of course, is awareness. Once you become aware of your governing relationship message, you can do something about it. And we have a way of helping you do just that. It has to do with respect — how much you respect yourself and how much you respect your partner.

This idea of respect brings us full circle, back to Part One of this book where we talked about uncovering your personal fear factor (whether it be the fear of losing time, approval, loyalty, or quality). This knowledge is the foundation of every great conversation. And when you invite respect to take part in your understanding of your own fear factor as well as your partner's, your governing relationship message takes a quantum leap in quality because respect ensures emotional safety.

The dictionary defines *respect* as a feeling of appreciation, honor, and esteem. "Respect is the younger brother of love," according to an English proverb. It creates a sense of security, as well as admiration and gratitude. When you respect yourself, you feel worthwhile. And when you respect your partner, you hold him or her in high regard.

Your internal dialogue, when you respect your partner, sounds like this: *I'm so thankful he is my partner; I really admire the way she lives her life; I know my partner's personal safety need and I want to honor it; I'm a better person because of my spouse.*

And when you respect yourself, your internal dialogue sounds like this: *I feel good about the kind of partner I am; I respect myself enough to let him know how I feel even if he doesn't agree; I'm still worthwhile when I make mistakes; I need to be true to who I am and own my personal safety need; my partner is a better person because I'm in his life.*

Exercise 19: Testing Your Respect Levels

Want to drill down a little deeper into your governing relationship message? This exercise provides a respect test that is sure to shed light on your internal dialogue. It will help you quantify your self-respect and your partner respect. But don't worry, it's not a threatening exercise; it's simply designed to raise your level of awareness so you can make improvements if needed.

Monitoring and Improving Your Inner Voice

If you were to sum up all your self-talk statements as they speak to your relationship and put the negative ones on one side of the scale and the positive ones on the other, which would win out? Would it be positive? We hope so. For the more positive your governing relationship message, the more likely you are to respect your partner's safety need and thus enjoy Love Talk. But truth be told, one negative self-statement can do in dozens of positive ones if it is expressed at an important moment. That's why it is particularly valuable to monitor your inner voice in situations that often elicit a negative tone.

A telltale sign of self-sabotage occurs when what is happening to you doesn't jibe with what you expect. It's Friday night, and you want your husband to suggest a fun restaurant for dinner. After all, "a loving husband would want to make it easy on his wife and spend some time together." But the thought never crosses his mind, and you don't say a word because "he should initiate it." So you sling through the leftovers in the fridge and sit down to eat. "Maybe we'll still have a nice conversation," you say to yourself. But you feel crestfallen as your partner points to the salad across the kitchen table while feeding his face with a forkful of leftover spaghetti. You wanted to connect, but he's too busy slamming down his food like he's late for a flight. Actually, it's a game on TV. So you clam up because "a woman shouldn't have to ask her partner to talk to her." On top of that, you're saying to yourself, "If he really cared about me, he'd want to find out how I'm doing." So your personal fear factor of losing his loyalty kicks in and you throw a pity party on your side of the kitchen table — and he doesn't even notice. "I'll take my ice cream in the family room," he says as he slides out of his chair, still gnawing on a breadstick.

> Feelings of worth can flourish only in an atmosphere where individual differences are appreciated, mistakes are tolerated, communication is open, and rules are flexible.
> Virginia Satir

You just sit there, feeling rejected and depressed. Sulking. Then you quietly mutter to yourself: "So much for devotion." All the while your self-respect is taking a nosedive while your partner respect plummets.

Let's take a good look at your self-talk in this situation. If you were to monitor it, you'd soon realize that you were being your own worst enemy. Your goal was to connect with your partner and see some evidence of devotion on his part, but you ended up trying to punish him for not initiating a conversation. You wanted to reprimand him for being in a hurry to watch a game instead of talking to you. In the end, you only punished yourself.

But how would your mood have changed if you'd said to yourself, "I can't expect him to read my mind — he doesn't know I'd like to go out tonight and enjoy a conversation." Or "Just because he doesn't initiate a conversation in this moment doesn't mean he's not interested in me and devoted to our relationship." Sure, it may take some mental muscle to conjure these thoughts, but aren't they more accurate? More rational?

This kind of self-talk increases your self-respect and your partner respect. With a more rational internal dialogue, you feel empowered to say aloud something like, "I really want to go out to eat tonight and just spend some time together." You make your desires known. There's no guessing game. No mind reading. And you respect your partner in the process. You don't paint him in to a mental corner that only you know about.

The point is that relational self-talk hangs on two hinges: self-respect and partner respect. And the more you cultivate both of them, the more you will honor each other's personal fear factors and enjoy the ease of

Love Talk.

What to Say When You Talk to Yourself

The following self-statements are time-tested to bolster your self-respect and partner respect. So be sure to throw some of these one-liners or questions into your internal dialogue.

- "How would I feel if I were in my partner's shoes right now?"
- "I want to keep my partner's personal safety need in mind."
- "Nobody's perfect — including my partner and me."
- "One of the things I appreciate most about my partner today is . . ."
- "If I'm not feeling appreciated, it may be because I'm not being appreciative."
- "What one thing could I do today to be a better partner?"
- "I can't always choose what happens to me, but I can always choose how I respond to it."

Talking from Your Strengths

If you are feeling even the slightest bit of discouragement, if you are feeling like you have some serious work to do, we want to leave you with an encouraging word. You are closer to enjoying Love Talk than you think.

Take a lesson from the world of business. Every savvy business executive knows success begins when you capitalize on what you do best. In fact, the most successful companies in the world today build their entire enterprise around the strengths of each individual employee. As they often say, the real tragedy for any company is not that its employees don't have the right strengths, but that they fail to use the strengths they have.

The same can be said of a relationship. We can become so consumed with our deficits that we neglect our strengths completely. We become what Benjamin Franklin called "sundials in the shade." That's the danger of negative self-talk — about you or your partner. So we want to leave you with a concrete opportunity to put your energies into affirming what you both do well so you will see a quantum leap in both your self-respect and your partner respect. At first you may think it sounds elementary and perfunctory, but we have seen it work wonders for countless couples, as they maximize their strengths and watch their Love Talk flourish. So we urge you to take it seriously.

Here's how it works: First, make a list of a half dozen things you appreciate about your partner. Take the time to ponder this and write them down. It is essential that you be as specific as possible and focus on character traits — not just what he or she does for you. For example, you may enjoy the way your partner leaves you kind notes or cute voicemail messages, but the underlying character trait may be that he is affectionate. You may appreciate the way your spouse picks up your mail, but the underlying character trait may be that she is thoughtful. You may appreciate the fact that your husband always pays your bills on time, but the character trait may be that he is disciplined. You get the idea. Consider admirable traits such as being:

- affectionate
- cheerful
- committed
- compassionate
- confident
- creative
- devout
- elegant
- energetic
- faithful

- generous
- gentle
- honest
- kind
- optimistic

This is just to get you started. You can add your own traits to this list. For each character trait you identify, it is helpful to note two or three examples of how you typically notice it in your partner.

We highly recommend that you consider your partner's strengths in these categories: mental, social, physical, and spiritual. Every partner wants to feel mentally capable, socially desirable, physically attractive, and spiritually vital, so consider comments that would boost your partner's self-respect in each of these areas. If these categories don't work for you, that's fine. The main goal is to make a list of the half dozen things you appreciate most about your partner.

Give yourself some time to construct this list, but once you have it, we guarantee that your partner would love to see it. In fact, this is crucial to improving your mutual respect. We suggest you set aside a specific time as a couple to share your lists. Make it a relationship summit for just the two of you. It could prove to be the most important meeting you attend all year!

Exercise 20: Talking from Your Strengths

This workbook exercise may be the most important one you do. It is designed to help you specifically drill down into what you and your partner do exceptionally well. So many couples sidestep taking an inventory of their own strengths to work on their deficits and get terribly bogged down because of them. Don't allow yourselves to skip this valuable exercise. Use the detailed chart in your workbooks.

Once you have both taken the time to complete your lists, be intentional about sharing them with each other. By the way, as you hear your spouse recount his or her list of admirable qualities about you, don't feel compelled to comment. And certainly don't discount them. This is a time to simply soak the compliments in.

The real value of this exercise is found in keeping your lists handy — the one you made for your partner and the one your partner made for you. Put them in your wallet. Place them on your desk. This will help you time and again in your efforts to boost your self-respect and partner-respect. As you review your list from time to time, it will keep you playing to your strengths. This simple exercise is the most effective way we have ever found to improve and maintain your positive self-talk.

> Feelings are simply what we say to ourselves about our experiences.
> Charles T. Brown

By the way, this exercise doesn't end there. Every few months, we suggest you revisit and revise your lists. Mark Twain said he could live for two months on a good compliment. That may be a good time frame in which to update your list of affirmations. The point is to keep it fresh.

So Remember This

The quiet conversation taking place in your head determines the closeness or distance you feel with each other. When your positive statements dwarf the negative, you're speaking Love Talk. When you remember your partner's personal fear factor and respect his or her emotional safety need, you are speaking Love Talk. When you intentionally respect and honor the hard-wiring of your partner's talk style, you are speaking Love Talk. When you put yourself in your partner's shoes with plenty of empathy, you are speaking Love Talk. When you keep your gender differences in mind and listen with the third ear, you are speaking Love Talk. When you do any and all of these, you are speaking Love Talk. Fluently.

EPILOGUE:
THE ULTIMATE MESSAGE
OF LOVE TALK

Aoccdrnig to rscheearch at Cmabrigde Uinervtisy, it deosn't mttaer in waht oredr the ltteers in a wrod are; the olny iprmoetnt tihng is taht the frist and lsat ltteer be at the rghit pclae. The rset can be a toatl mses and you can sitll raed it wouthit porbelm. Tihs is bcuseae the huamn mnid deos not raed ervey lteter by istlef, but the wrod as a wlohe.

Okay, before you fire off an email to the publisher about the inexcusable lack of proofreading for typos on this page, we want to be sure you read through the entire paragraph so you get the point. That point being that even with a lot of errors you can still communicate very effectively.

We leave you with this little amazement because it reveals an important lesson for every couple who wants to enjoy Love Talk: the best communicators give each other permission to make mistakes, because you are both bound to make them (not even the most studied experts hold a perfect record), and life together is a whole lot sweeter when your communication errors are received with grace.

Every once in a while at one of our relationship seminars around the country, we will hear couples talking over the lunch hour or during a break and one of them will say, "Hey, you're not listening to me the way they said to do it," or "You're not clarifying my content the way we just learned." That always makes us cringe. The point is not to be perfect, to never color outside the lines. It's not to catch your spouse in error. The point is to connect.

Think of it this way: we've given you the best tools we have for speaking each other's language — for making the deepest verbal connection possible. You've read the book, talked about its principles, and taken the self-tests. Now it's time to put what you've learned into practice. What this research at Cambridge University shows us is that each of us is hardwired to make sense of communication mistakes. That's good news — very good news — for all who long to speak Love Talk! When we are willing to look beyond errors, we have a leg up on every inevitable communication meltdown.

This book will not make you perfect communicators at every turn. We're the first to admit it. You are guaranteed to still have times when you feel completely misunderstood. Times when you hear something your partner is saying in a way it was never intended. You are sure to have times when your partner is treating a subject too lightly or too seriously. You are guaranteed to bump into moments when your partner is simply "not communicating right." And they are sure to find the same in you. That's life in a close relationship.

But in those times when your communication isn't smooth, allow your hardwiring to pass over any errors you might find — even the most glaring. Your mind is built to do just that if you give it a chance. But this means that when you've spotted your partner in error, you give up nitpicking and recoil your accusatory finger. Instead, focus on what you understand and what makes the most sense. This is sure to stifle your inner critic, get your communication back on track, and provide a space for each of you to breathe deep . . . and relax in the comfort of giving and receiving grace.

You don't have to be "prfeect communatocirs" to speak each other's language. Perfection has never been a prerequisite to profound connection. That's the ultimate message of Love Talk.

APPENDIX A:
PRACTICAL HELP FOR
THE SILENT PARTNER

Sticks and stones are hard on bones
Aimed with angry art,
Words can sting like anything,
But silence breaks the heart.
Phyllis McGinley

Working as a medical psychologist just out of grad school, I (Les) often consulted with physicians who were treating patients suffering from terrible physical burns. Because the healing process for burn patients is so excruciating and because the necessary treatment so painful, some burn patients simply cannot cope and give up trying. As nurses wheel them down the hall and into the tank room where they will be submerged so their burned skin can be meticulously scrubbed to prevent dangerous infections, the patients cry out, "Don't touch me. Just let me die!"

And it's no exaggeration to say that some

non-talkers feel the same way about the possibility of pain in their relationship.[1] They silently cry out: "Don't touch! Leave me alone." They've probably learned the hard way that vulnerability can be excruciating. They've had their heart kicked across the floor too many times. So they clam up, silently vowing never to open up again. They become a silent partner.

Yet inside, every silent partner knows that their healing will eventually call them to open up. It's the nature of love. "To love at all is to be vulnerable," writes C. S. Lewis in *The Four Loves.* "Love anything, and your heart will be wrung and possibly broken. If you want to be sure of keeping your heart intact — you must give your heart to no one, not even an animal. Wrap it carefully around with hobbies and little luxuries, avoid all entanglements. Lock it up safely in the casket of your selfishness. And in that casket, safe, dark, motionless, airless, it will not change, it will not be broken. It will become unbreakable, impenetrable, and irredeemable. The only place outside of heaven where you can be perfectly safe from the dangers of love is hell."

If you tend to be a non-talker, we want to encourage you. You don't have to keep living in a quiet casket of fear. You can love and be loved. Is it risky? Sure. But the following six-step plan has helped hundreds just like you weather the risk and reclaim a relationship characterized by Love Talk. So here goes.

1. Own Your Piece of the Pie

In 1990, when Bill McCartney founded Promise Keepers, the ministry dedicated to building men of integrity, he truly believed that his marriage to Lyndi was fine. His commitment to both coaching another stellar season at the University of Colorado and building up this new ministry, however, provided the perfect camouflage for hypocrisy in his personal life. "It may sound unbelievable," he writes in his book *Sold Out,* "but while Promise Keepers was spiritually inspiring to my core, my hard-charging approach to the ministry was distracting me from being in the truest sense, a promise keeper to my own family."

McCartney points to two events that showed him he was out of touch and avoiding responsibility for the condition of his own marriage. One was a Promise Keepers rally at which men were told to write down the number their wives would give their marriages if rating them on a scale of one to ten. He had to admit with embarrassment to the other men on the platform that Lyndi would probably only give their marriage a six.

Then in the fall of 1994, McCartney heard a speaker make this pointed statement: "If you want to know about a man's character, then look into the face of his wife. Whatever he has invested in or withheld from her will be reflected in her countenance." Something clicked in McCartney. As he puts it, he escorted his "wounded wife" out of the parking lot determined that rebuilding his marriage would require him to take drastic measures. Shortly thereafter, Coach McCartney announced his retirement from the University of Colorado in order to spend time with Lyndi. To do so, he gave up the ten years remaining on his $350,000-a-year contract. *Sports Illustrated* called it "un-American." McCartney called it taking responsibility for the state of his marriage.

The single best day in every relationship is when two partners take responsibility for their piece of the pie. This doesn't require anything as dramatic as quitting your job, but it can be just as scary. Taking ownership for your deficit — your non-talking ways — can be daunting, since once you take ownership, you are compelled to change. This must be what Nelson Mandela was thinking when he said, "Our greatest fear is not that we will discover that we are inadequate, but that we will discover that we are powerful beyond measure."

In the short run, it is far easier to avoid responsibility for our problems by blaming someone else. But in the long haul, owning up to your lack of empathy, your silent treatment, your self-sabotage is the single most important predictor of turning your Non-Talk into Love Talk.

2. Recognize Your Vulnerability

Achilles, the Greek mythological hero, was noted for his strength and bravery. In *The Iliad,* his mother, Thetis, had a premonition that her son would die in battle. So she dipped him in the River Styx to make him invulnerable. Thetis held the infant by his heel while the rest of his body was immersed in the water. As fate would have it, a poison arrow shot by Apollo wounded Achilles in the heel, his only vulnerable spot, and caused his death.

Chances are that non-talking is the Achilles' heel of your relationship. Outside of this one weakness, your relationship may afford more than you can ask. You may be financially secure, live in a good neighborhood, and have a warm circle of friends and wonderful kids. But until you protect your relationship from the vulnerability of Non-Talk, your relationship is in danger. We have seen more couples than we care to count whose relationships have collapsed — even though they had many positive qualities — because they never attended to this issue of Non-Talk.

So we urge you to recognize the seriousness of this deficit. Don't delude yourself into thinking it will disappear on its own. You've got to give it your attention. And we know that because you are reading this, you are doing just that. You're on your way.

3. Look Beyond Your Own Pain to Your Partner's

We know you probably have good reasons for retreating. You feel hurt. You've withstood an injustice you didn't deserve. Whatever your story, we don't want to demean it, but we do want to help you transcend it. So this step can be tough. It requires you to deliberately climb over your own pain in search of your partner's.

There is an old Chinese tale about a woman whose only son died. In her grief, she went to a holy man and asked, "What magical incantations do you have to bring my son back to life?" Instead of sending her away or reasoning with her, he said to her, "Fetch me a mustard seed from a home that has never known sorrow. We will use it to drive the sorrow out of your life."

The woman set off at once in search of that magical mustard seed. She came first to a splendid mansion, knocked at the door, and said, "I am looking for a home that has never known sorrow. Is this such a place? It is very important to me." They told her, "You've certainly come to the wrong place," and began to describe all the tragic things that had recently befallen them. The woman said to herself, "Who is better able to help these poor unfortunate people than I, who have had misfortune of my own?" She stayed to comfort them, then went on in her search for a home that had never known sorrow. But wherever she turned, in hovels and palaces, she found one report after another of sadness and misfortune. Ultimately, the woman became so involved in ministering to other people's grief that she forgot about her quest for the magical mustard seed, never realizing it had in fact driven the sorrow out of her life.

Once you make the choice to rise above your self-pity, once you give up on a magical cure for your conditions, you will find yourself with an entirely new outlook on life and love. You will see that your relationship is not only about getting your own needs met, but about meeting your mate's. Sure, you already know this in your head, but determine to bring your sluggish heart along with you. This will open the door of your life to empathy, and you will be in shock and awe by its transforming power.

4. Find Compassionate but Honest Feedback

Henry Ward Beecher said, "No man can tell another his faults so as to benefit him, unless he loves him." If you are to climb over your Non-Talk pattern and learn to empathize with your partner, you will find the journey much easier with a trusted guide, a mentor, or an accountability partner who will walk with you — not for the purpose of pointing out your faults, but because he wants the best for you.

So give serious consideration to a mentor or coach you can confide in — a person who will gently guide you as you work to get out of your Non-Talk rut and cut a new groove in your communication patterns. While this step can be difficult to take, we've discovered that it significantly speeds up the progress for most.

Approach a person you respect and ask him or her about a mentoring relationship that would enable you to learn more about how to be a loving spouse. Or you may even consider hiring a short-term life coach. Of course, being coached or mentored requires opening yourself to critical feedback. But a true coach will only give you a compassionate critique to help you become better. A mentoring relationship establishes a sense of accountability for improvement and is a vital element for anyone serious about changing his or her ways. Even the icon of non-talkers, Ebenezer Scrooge, in Charles Dickens' *A Christmas Carol,* had a "mentor" in Jacob Marley's ghost. Through their relationship, the miserly old man exclaimed, "I will not be the man I was," and he wasn't.

5. Experiment with Vulnerability

There is no way around it: when we open up to another person, we risk rejection and disappointment. Just as a child risks scraping a knee when learning to ride a bike, so do you and I risk emotional pain when entering into vulnerable dialogue. Now don't misunderstand. We're not asking you to bare your soul at the deepest level. We're simply suggesting that you try an experiment. The opening up about a project at work, for example, that you would normally keep mum about. Tell your partner how it is making you feel. Say something like, "I have this deadline at work that is really weighing heavily on me." Then see what happens.

If you don't get the response from your partner you'd like, that's okay. It happens to all of us. Let it go for the moment. Don't allow it to shut you down. Chances are, if you are looking for a specific response, you are going to feel hurt on some of these occasions. It's part of the process. As psychiatrist and author M. Scott Peck has said, "We cannot heal without being willing to be hurt."

Peck also has said, "If Jesus taught us anything, he taught us that the way to salvation lies through vulnerability."[2] So take the risk of opening yourself to your partner. Disclose what you can to him or her. The effect of vulnerability on a spouse is almost always disarming. Vulnerability begets vulnerability. And it's this give and take that builds the bridge over the troubled waters of Non-Talk.

6. Seek Healing through Professional Help

Finally, if you are entrenched in a deep rut of Non-Talk, you are probably pretty wounded. And those wounds may have absolutely nothing to do with your partner. We'll never forget speaking to several hundred married marines who had just returned from fighting in Iraq. They had been away from their spouses for months on end. And believe us when we say this group had more than its share of non-talkers. But these silent partners were not clamming up because of their mates; it was the hellish experience they had just endured.

Well, you don't have to go to war to suffer wounds. You may have grown up in a home that inflicted plenty of emotional or physical pain. You may have suffered a wrenching career twist. You may have been burned in a previous relationship. Whatever the source of your splintered self-esteem, if you are carrying around pain that is interfering with your relationship, we urge you to seek the help of a competent counselor. Ask others in the helping profession if they know of a good referral. Physicians, ministers, nurses, and teachers often provide excellent referrals. Other informational sources include hospitals, community service societies, referral services, and local professional societies. This final step may be the most important thing you ever do for yourself and your relationship.

APPENDIX B:
SAMPLE REPORT

LOVE TALK INDICATOR

Name: Jane Smith

You are now in possession of your *Love Talk Indicator Individual Report* — the most powerful communication assessment for identifying, understanding, and maximizing your talk style within your relationship. In this report, you will receive the following important pieces of information:

- Your Fear Factor Index
- Your Personal Love Talk Profile
- Detailed Summary of Your Personal Talk Style
- Keys to Love Talk: How You Like Your Partner to Talk to You
- Barriers to Love Talk: What Your Partner Needs to Know about How Not to Talk to You

- Love Talk Tips: What You Need to Do When Talking to Your Partner

The information you will read about yourself in this report will lay a solid foundation for enjoying Love Talk with your partner. Of course, **to truly take your conversations to the next level and beyond, you will make the most of this information when your partner takes the Love Talk Indicator as well.** Once your partner does this, a Love Talk Couple's Report will be generated for the two of you, building significantly on your Individual Report and giving you additional detailed information tailored specifically to the combination of your two styles. For example, you will learn the specific signs that will trigger your partner's "fear factor." And you'll obtain personalized tips on how you can both make each other feel emotionally safe. This information is the essence of Love Talk. It's what enables you to speak each other's language like you never have before.

Your partner can take the Love Talk Indicator at www.RealRelationships.com. Once you see what the Combined Couple's Report does for your communication, you'll quickly see why the Love Talk Indicator is the most powerful communication tool you'll ever encounter. Your conversations will never be the same.

With every good wish,

Les & Leslie

Your Fear Factor Index

Pin-pointing your personal "fear factor" — the one area that tends to cause you the most emotional unease or even anxiety in your daily conversations — is a major step toward enjoying Love Talk. This is your top emotional safety need. It's what helps you feel most safe and secure when talking with your partner. According to your responses on the Love Talk Indicator, here is a graphical index prioritizing what makes you feel most emotionally safe (the first one being your most powerful need).

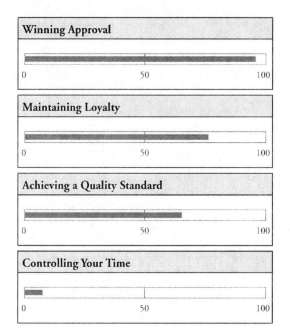

Your Love Talk Profile

The following profile depicts your approach to the four fundamental domains of conversation: (1) How you tackle problems (aggressively or passively); (2) How you influence your partner (with facts or feelings); (3) How you react to change (with resistance or acceptance); and (4) How you make decisions (cautiously or spontaneously). Here are your four scores graphically illustrated, starting with your strongest conversational dimension.

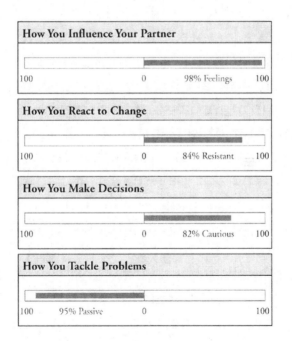

How You Influence Your Partner		
100	0	98% Feelings	100

How You React to Change		
100	0	84% Resistant	100

How You Make Decisions		
100	0	82% Cautious	100

How You Tackle Problems		
100	95% Passive	0	100

Your Love Talk Style

Below you will find a summary of your personal talk style. This report is unique and specific to you and is based on how you responded to the Love Talk Indicator. It reveals your natural leanings. Focus on those statements that describe you best and discuss those with your partner to begin creating a Love Talk environment. The more accurately he understands your conversational hardwiring (and the more you understand yourself), the easier it will be for you to speak each other's language like you never have before. Because your top emotional safety need is winning your partner's approval, you are rarely quick to confront. This communicates a strong message to your partner of being devoted and dedicated to him. You are unlikely to disagree with your partner or say no to a request from your partner as long as you continue to feel valued and connected. However, if you lose your sense of connectedness and loyalty, you are likely to withdraw and become passive in your conversations.

In conversations with your partner you also tend to retreat when confronted. You are prone to defer and lack assertiveness when the two of you talk.

Again, since winning approval from your

partner is a high emotional safety need for you, you may not always keep your partner fully informed of issues that matter to him. You may put off having a conversation that should have taken place earlier.

Your tendency to influence your partner with feelings more than facts causes you to engender optimism in your relationship. Your perception is that the glass is half-full rather than half-empty. You also have a natural interest in people. Therefore, when you and your partner are in social situations, your partner may feel that on occasion others become more important to you than he is. In other words, your partner may feel left out of the conversation.

Your cooperative and easygoing style stems from your low score on the emotional safety need to control time. Your lack of urgency allows you to be more mild-mannered and more unassuming in your conversations. You go along instead of make waves. Even when you are in the midst of a serious conversation with your partner, you still like to have fun. You may interject humor to alleviate tension and to indicate your optimistic outlook in the solution of the issue. If your partner is not in a mood to play, this can communicate a lack of serious attention and can lead to occasional friction.

In conversations with your partner, you do not mind following your partner's lead. This willingness to take the back seat is probably derived from your strong sense of loyalty. You may even tend to find emotional security from your partner when he is strong and decisive in your conversations.

When making plans with your partner, you will display discernment and a good sense of timing. This helps you to bring up the right issues at the right time.

At times, you may be hesitant in making decisions with your partner. Your need to collect information to make a wise decision can cause you to come off as overly cautious and indecisive.

More than likely, you have conversations with your partner around balancing your home life with your career or even your social calendar. In other words, your need for approval can lead you to devote time to activities that pull you away from your relationship with your partner. While this issue relates to many couples, your hardwiring makes this particularly important for you and is bound to be a point of tension in your conversations.

If you are emotionally attached to an issue

in your conversation, you can display a tremendous sense of urgency around resolving a problem associated with that issue. Once the problem is solved, however, you will tend to readily move on to the next activity.

Your cooperative style of conversation keeps you from declaring your intentions immediately. You often feel a need to weigh the pros and cons in any given situation before declaring your opinion, revealing your thoughts, or making a commitment.

Because you do not want to lose your partner's approval, you can sometimes say what your partner wants to hear in order to diffuse potential conflict in a conversation. This is normally founded on good intentions, but it can lead to inaction since you said something in the moment to relieve the tension rather than to root out the problem and find a real solution. If you find yourself revisiting the same issue repeatedly in your conversations, this could be the case.

One of your great strengths is your ability to generate a sense of warmth in your conversations. You tend to be an enthusiastic person in your conversations and this can become contagious. In other words, this quality can lead your partner to become involved in activities or conversations simply because you are.

Keys to Love Talk

A central component of Love Talk is identifying how you most like your partner to communicate with you. Below you will find a list of items that are specific to you. You will resonate with some items on this list more than others. After reviewing the list, identify your top four items and explore them with your partner.

How You Like Your Partner to Talk to You
- Ease off the gas pedal and relax whenever possible.
- Talk about your personal expectations, making them known early on.
- Give specific compliments (e.g., "I love the way you said that").
- Offer opinions and ideas that bolster a connection between you.
- Be prepared to listen to stories — for the mere enjoyment of the story.
- Let her know you hear her feelings as well as her words.
- Invite her into your world by asking her opinion on issues of concern.
- Take time to unpack her thinking and feelings.
- Use a tone of voice that shows sincerity and care.

- Let her know what's on your mind and what might be troubling you.

Barriers to Love Talk

Another aspect to enjoying Love Talk is learning what to avoid in your conversations together. This section of the report describes for your partner specifically what NOT to do when communicating with you. Again, you are likely to resonate with some of these items more than others. After reviewing the list, identify your top four items and explore them with your partner.

What Your Partner Needs to Know about How NOT to Talk to You

- Don't talk down (e.g., "You wouldn't understand.").
- Don't rush into decision-making without consulting her.
- Don't stick to your agenda too rigidly or be overly time-conscious.
- Don't be self-centered or demanding in your requests.
- Don't confront aggressively.
- Don't make promises you can't keep.
- Don't be dogmatic or unbending (e.g., "I'm done. End of discussion.").
- Don't be cool, aloof, or tight-lipped with information.
- Don't push too hard or be unrealistic with expectations.
- Don't be random, rambling, or hap-

hazard in the presentation of ideas.
- Don't hide your emotions or feelings from her.

Love Talk Tips

The next major key to enjoying Love Talk with your partner — a crucial key to unlocking the kinds of conversations you want most — is accurately identifying his top emotional safety needs. **Once he takes the Love Talk Indicator (LTI) you will know specifically how your two "fear factors" uniquely combine.** Until then, here are a few quick suggestions to give your partner to help him understand more about how to talk to you.

If your partner is a person who is patient, predictable, reliable, steady, relaxed, and modest, it is likely that your partner's top emotional safety need is **maintaining loyalty and devotion.**

If this describes your partner, here are a few suggestions on how to create more Love Talk:

- Begin with a personal comment to break the ice.
- Present your case softly, minimizing any threat to your connection.
- Ask "how" questions to draw out her opinions.

Factors that will create tension or dissatisfaction in your conversations with your partner:

- Moving into "problem-solving mode" before making a personal connection.
- Being domineering or demanding.
- Forcing her to respond quickly to your objectives.

If she is systematic, neat, conservative, perfectionist, careful, and compliant, it is likely that your partner's top emotional safety need is **achieving quality standards.**

If this describes your partner, here are a few suggestions on how to create more Love Talk:

- Prepare your "case" in advance.
- Stick to business.
- Be accurate and realistic.

Factors that will create tension or dissatisfaction in your conversations with your partner:

- Being giddy, casual, informal, or loud.
- Pushing too hard or being unrealistic with deadlines.
- Being disorganized or messy.

If your partner is a person who is ambitious, forceful, decisive, strong-willed, independent, and goal-oriented, it is likely that your partner's top emotional safety need is **gaining control of her time.**

If this describes your partner, here are a few general suggestions on how to create more Love Talk:

- Be clear, specific, brief, and to the point.
- Stick to the topic or agenda.
- Be prepared with support material in a well-organized package.

Factors that will create tension or dissatisfaction in your conversations with your partner:

- Talking about things that are not relevant to the issue or task at hand.
- Leaving loopholes, unfinished thoughts, or decisions hanging in the air.
- Appearing disorganized or uninformed.

If she is magnetic, enthusiastic, friendly, demonstrative, and polished, it is likely that your partner's top emotional safety need **is winning the approval of others.**

If this describes your partner, here are a few general suggestions on how to create more Love Talk:

- Provide a warm and friendly environment.
- Don't deal with a lot of details (put them in writing).
- Ask "feeling" questions to draw out her opinions or comments.

Factors that will create tension or dissatisfaction in your conversations with your partner:

- Being curt, cold, or tight-lipped.
- Controlling the conversation.
- Blindsiding her with a confrontational message.

Please keep in mind that this is only a general overview and merely hints at what you will both gain from the Couple's Report (CR). The CR combines each of your personal LTI results into one in-depth summary — tailored specifically to the two of you — and guides you step-by-step through a personalized process for more Love Talk. We hope you will take this important next step.

NOTES

Chapter One: Can We Talk?

1. By the way, we were motivated in our pursuit of deeper and lasting communication keys from a professional perspective as well as a personal one. Research shows that when divorced couples are asked about the cause, 5% say it was due to physical abuse, 16% due to drug or alcohol abuse, and 17% due to adultery. The overwhelming cause of divorce reported by those who went through it was "incompatibility" — failure to simply get along together. As one report of these findings puts it, "Stated differently, three-fifths of marriages failed due to poor communication or conflict resolution skills" (M. McManus, "How to Create an America That Saves Marriages," *Journal of Psychology and Theology* 31 [2003]: 203) — reason enough for any marriage counselor to want to thoroughly understand com-

munication training for couples.

Chapter Two: Relational Lifeblood

1. B. J. Fowers, "Psychology and the good marriage: Social theory as practice," *American Behavioral Scientist* 41 (1998): 516–26.
2. R. M. Sabatelli, R. Buck, and A. Dreyer, "Nonverbal Communication Accuracy in Married Couples," *Journal of Personality and Social Psychology* 43, no. 5 (1982): 1088–97.
3. 1 Corinthians 13:1.

Chapter Three: Communication 101

1. See, for example, Job 19:2–3.

Chapter Four: The Foundation of Every Great Conversation

1. J. Scott Armstrong, "Bafflegab Pays," *Psychology Today* (May 1980), 12.
2. See W. M. Marston, *The Emotions of Normal People* (1928; repr., Minneapolis: Persona Press, 1979); W. Clark, *The Activity Vector Analysis: Basic theory, administration, and application of activity vector analysis* (Barrington, RI: Walter V. Clarke Associates, 1967); B. J. Bonnstetter, J. Suiter, and R. J. Widrick, *DISC: A Reference Manual* (Scottsdale, AZ: Target Train-

ing International, 1993); B. J. Bonnstetter, J. Suiter, and R. J. Widrick, *The Universal Language: DISC* (Scottsdale, AZ: Target Training International, 2001); M. O'Connor, *The DISC Model, Trainer and Consultant Reference Encyclopedia* (New York: Life Associates, 1987); C. G. Jung, Gerhard Adler, R. F. C. Hull, *Psychological Types,* Collected Works of C. G. Jung, vol. 6 (Princeton, NJ: Princeton University Press, 1971); J. Trent, R. A. Cox, and E. S. Tooker, *Leading From Your Strengths* (Nashville: Broadman and Holman, 2004).

3. Sidebar in *U.S. News & World Report* (January 20, 1989).

4. M. Raphael, "It's True: Drivers Move Slowly If You Want Their Space," *Raleigh News and Observer* (May 13, 1997), 1A.

5. "What's Inside a Real-Life Panic Room?" ABCnews.com (accessed April 2, 2004).

Chapter Six: How Do You Influence Each Other?

1. Wesley Britton, "Mark Twain: 'Cradle Skeptic,' " www.yorku.ca (accessed April 2, 2004).

2. Susan K. Harris, "The Courtship of Olivia Langdon and Mark Twain," *Cambridge Studies in American Literature and*

Culture (Cambridge: Cambridge University Press, 1996), xiii.

Chapter Seven: How Do You React to Change?

1. Hans Finzel, *Change Is Like a Slinky: 30 Strategies for Promoting and Surviving Change in Your Organization* (Chicago: Northfield, 2004).

Chapter Eight: How Do You Make Decisions?

1. K. Kersting, "Cons of Perfectionism Include Self-Criticism," *Monitor on Psychology,* May 2004, 20.
2. C. Yeager, *Chuck Yeager* (New York: Bantam, 1985).

Chapter Ten: Talking a Fine Line

1. John Gottman, "Welcome to the Love Lab," *Psychology Today* (Sept. 2000), 42–48.
2. For a summary on the value of empathy in each of these domains, see D. Goleman, *Emotional Intelligence* (New York: Bantam, 1995); and H. Weisinger, *Emotional Intelligence at Work* (San Francisco: Jossey-Bass, 1998).
3. B. Azar, "Defining the Trait That Makes Us Human," *APA Monitor* 28 (1997): 1.

Chapter Eleven: Men Analyze, Women Sympathize

1. D. Tannen, ed., *Framing in Discourse* (Oxford and New York: Oxford University Press, 1993), 358.
2. C. Hall and J. Mosemak, "USA Snapshots," *USA Today,* April 30, 1997, A1.
3. Reported in Barbara and Allan Pease, *Why Men Don't Listen and Women Can't Read Maps* (New York: Welcome Rain Publishers, 2000).
4. Robert Bly, quoted in Gloria Bird and Michael Sporakowski, *Taking Sides: Clashing Views on Controversial Issues in Family and Personal Relationships,* 3rd ed. (Guildford, CT: William C. Brown Publishers, 1996).
5. R. J. Watson and Peter T. Klassen, *Style Insights DISC Instrument Validation Manual* (Scottsdale, AZ: Target Training International, 2004).
6. Ibid.
7. L. R. Brody and J. A. Hall, "Gender and Emotion," in Michael Lewis and Jeanette M. Haviland-Jones, eds., *Handbook of Emotions* (New York: Guilford Press, 1993).
8. D. Tannen, *You Just Don't Understand* (New York: Ballantine, 1991).
9. C. Gilligan, *In a Different Voice: Psycho-*

logical Theory and Women's Development (Cambridge: Harvard University Press, 1982).

Chapter Twelve: Listening with the Third Ear

1. E. Foulke, "Listening Comprehension as a Function of Word Rate," *Journal of Communication* 18 (1968): 198.
2. N. L. Van Pelt, *How to Speak So Your Mate Will Listen and Listen So Your Mate Will Speak* (Grand Rapids: Revell, 1989).
3. V. P. Richmond, J. C. McCroskey, and K. D. Roach, "Communication and decision-making styles, power base usage, and satisfaction in marital dyads," *Communication Quarterly* 4 (1997): 410–17.
4. E. Stotland, *Empathy, Fantasy and Helping,* "Sage Library of Social Research," vol. 65 (London: Sage, 1978), 179.
5. Deborah Tannen uses this example in her helpful book, *I Only Say This Because I Love You* (New York: Random House, 2001), 8.
6. M. Purdy and D. Borishoff, eds., *Listening in Everyday Life* (New York: University of America Press, 1996).
7. Paul Tournier, *To Understand Each Other* (Atlanta: John Knox Press, 1967), 29.

Chapter Fourteen: Let's Talk Love

1. It was customary in China to marry children but have them remain with their parents until they were older — a custom that contributed to this couple's extremely long marriage.
2. D. E. Conroy and J. N. Metzler, "Patterns of Self-Talk Associated with Different Forms of Competitive Anxiety," *Journal of Sport and Exercise Psychology* 26 (2003): 69–87.
3. S. Helmstetter, *What to Say When You Talk to Yourself* (New York: Fine Communications, 1997).
4. Much of our thinking about self-talk was shaped by the research Les conducted with Dr. Neil Clark Warren in their book, *Love the Life You Live* (Tyndale, 2003) and found in the chapter titled "Tuning Into Your Self-Talk."
5. B. H. Levine, *Your Body Believes Every Word You Say: The Language of the Body/ Mind Connection* (Boulder Creek, CA: Aslan, 1991).
6. S. Blakeslee, "Tracing the Brain's Pathways for Linking Emotion and Reason," *New York Times,* December 6, 1994, B1.
7. C. P. Neck and C. C. Manz, "Thought Self-leadership: The Influence of Self-talk and Mental Imagery on Performance,

Journal of Organizational Behavior 13 (1992): 681–99.

8. L. Ievleva and T. Orlick, "Mental Links to Enhanced Healing: An Exploratory Study," *The Sport Psychologist* 5 (1991): 25–40.

Appendix A: A Practical Help for the Silent Partner

1. C. Flora, "The Blirtacious Wives Club," *Psychology Today,* March 2004, 22.

2. M. Scott Peck, *The Road Less Traveled* (1978; repr. New York: Simon and Schuster, 2002).

ABOUT THE AUTHORS

Drs. Les Parrott and **Leslie Parrott** are codirectors of the Center for Relationships Development at Seattle Pacific University (SPU), a groundbreaking program dedicated to teaching the basics of good relationships. Les Parrott is a professor of clinical psychology at SPU, and Leslie is a marriage and family therapist at SPU. The Parrotts are authors of the Gold Medallion Award–winning *Saving Your Marriage Before It Starts, Becoming Soul Mates, The Love List, Relationships,* and *When Bad Things Happen to Good Marriages.* They have been featured on *Oprah, CBS This Morning,* CNN, and *The View,* and in *USA Today* and the *New York Times.* They are also frequent guest speakers and have written for a variety of magazines. The Parrotts' radio program, *Love Talk,* can be heard on stations throughout North America. They live in Seattle, Washington, with their two sons.

4/13 -H
10/13 D
3116 W

9 781594 154539